TikTok Boom

Chris Stokel-Walker

Also by Chris Stokel-Walker

*YouTubers: How YouTube Shook Up TV and
Created a New Generation of Stars* (Canbury Press)

TikTok Boom

China's Dynamite App and
the Superpower Race for Social Media

Chris Stokel-Walker

 sourcebooks

Published by Sourcebooks
P.O. Box 4410, Naperville, Illinois 60567-4410
(630) 961-3900
sourcebooks.com

Originally published as *TikTok Boom* in 2021 in Great Britain by Canbury Press,
an imprint of Canbury Press. This edition issued based on the paperback edition
published in 2021 in Great Britain by Canbury Press, an imprint of Canbury Press.

Printed and bound in the United States of America.
POD

CONTENTS

INTRODUCTION

Andy Warhol's idea that anyone can be famous for 15 minutes has never looked shakier. In the programme for an exhibition in Stockholm in 1968, the American pop art pioneer wrote: 'In the future, everyone will be world-famous for 15 minutes.' What struck many at the time as an outlandish prediction is in danger of being undercut by reality in the third decade of the 21st Century. On TikTok, anyone with a mobile phone can become known to hundreds of millions of people for a matter of seconds, and then slip back into anonymity. True, a run of successful self-shot videos can propel an individual from an everyday life into that of a multi-millionaire. Unlike in Warhol's age, however, the metamorphosis from ordinariness to fame occurs not through the multiple media channels of Andy Warhol's age, but through a single, super-fast, ever-mutating social media app. Which is ultimately owned in China and ruled over by an inscrutable algorithm.

Existing celebrity doesn't determine success on TikTok. 'Anyone has the potential to go viral on TikTok. You can have one follower or a million followers,' says Yazmin How, chief of TikTok's

UK editorial team. It meets at 9am daily to review some of the 1.6 million videos uploaded to TikTok in the UK every 24 hours. (Only 9% of users post videos; the remainder just watch them.) How and her colleagues' accounts have been stripped of the highly powerful algorithm, which serves up content according to a person's viewing history and interests. It's the God's eye view of TikTok, drinking straight from the gush of videos being posted every single day.

TikTok's algorithm works on what's called a 'content graph', looking at what you've previously engaged with, rather than a 'social graph' – which accounts you follow. That makes it possible for a video to go super-viral from less than super surroundings. 'We see things going viral all the time from people who have maybe, like, 50 fans, who crack something,' says How. 'There's no recipe for it. There's no magic formula.'

Such unpredictability makes the churn of celebrities through TikTok so speedy. They're people like Curtis Roach, whose rap about being stuck at home during the pandemic turned him from someone with $12 to his name to a celebrity musician, or Nathan Evans, a Scottish postman whose sea shanties landed him a record deal that many would kill for. One minute these people were just like you and me. Then they were put up on a digital pedestal, admired and envied the world over.

This book is about these 'no-one to someone' videomakers – 'creators' – but it also tells the story of TikTok's rise and the impact it's having on society, from pop music to politics. And more... because to view TikTok as just the platform is to miss the bigger debate. Yes, TikTok's rise is meteoric. Yes, it's creating a new generation of celebrities – many of whom are younger than the YouTubers who came before them. But the rise of TikTok has wider ramifications, arising from the fact that it was made by, and is still owned by, a Chinese company. Having spent so long merely making phones and computers for Western companies, China is now rapidly pushing into software and artificial intelligence. Beijing plans to spend more than $1.4 trillion in the next five years developing next-generation technologies. The country has goals beyond its borders, and TikTok is caught up in a debate held in capitals across the globe whether the short form video sharing app is a Trojan horse for a bigger tech invasion from East (Communist China in particular and Asia more generally) to West (chiefly the capitalist economies of the USA and Europe). Or whether it's simply a private company trying to become a mainstay in a world previously dominated by big companies in a 130 square kilometre parcel of land in the San Francisco Bay in California, better known as Silicon Valley. The two sides of the argument are entrenched and far apart.

TikTok has mutated into something of a proxy war over the future of the technology we rely on in our everyday lives. And the outcome could potentially dictate the future direction of the apps we install on our phones, and where our data goes. For the last 20 years, Westerners have knowingly handed over the most intimate details of our lives, from our favourite brand of pasta to our illnesses to our underwear size, to the GAFA companies based in the United States (Google, Apple, Facebook and Amazon). It's a trust that successive scandals have shown to be misplaced. TikTok's origins lie elsewhere, in a country Westerners fear would more willingly sacrifice personal rights to protect its national interests. With increasing amounts of our lives being transacted online, does it matter if our data and our money stays within the control of a few firms in Silicon Valley or starts to migrate to data servers controlled by companies ultimately run out of China?

Politicians outside China certainly seem to think so, which is why TikTok, alongside Huawei and other Chinese innovations, have become the subjects of searching criticism and investigations in the West. TikTok was thrust squarely into the sights of Donald Trump, who, while the US President in 2020, decided to make a short-form video-sharing app – beloved by teens for lip-syncing pop songs – the enemy in a national security investigation, with billion-dollar business consequences. At the same time, parallel investigations in India, Japan, Australia, Europe and the United Kingdom were delving into whether TikTok was, despite the analyses of multiple cyber-security experts, secreting information to Chinese spies. Politicians have shown they will act, too: India banned TikTok in June 2020, alongside 58 other apps developed within China's borders – a move made permanent in January 2021, leaving a dedicated audience of 200 million users without a home, and thousands of employees without a job.

Unsurprisingly, given the growth and power of its business, TikTok is fighting back, in the US and elsewhere. After a steady rumble of discontent that grew into deliberate PR campaigns warning that it was becoming a pawn in a broader geopolitical battle, the company protested that 'the [Trump] Administration paid no attention to facts, dictated terms of an agreement without going through standard legal processes, and tried to insert itself into negotiations between private businesses.' Less than three weeks later, TikTok filed a lawsuit against the US President, alleging he had run roughshod over normal governmental practice and the first and fifth amendments in order to score political points and jeopardise the future of a new driver of the global economy. What was once the story of an enormously popular app's impact on our online and offline culture had been hurled into a tussle between the world's two biggest superpowers.

This book, then, tells the story of TikTok, where it came from and how it has transformed our society and taken over the world. With the help of those who've been intimately acquainted with the inner workings of TikTok, you'll learn how the company operates, what its goals are, and where it's going. You'll discover the complicated lineage of the world's fastest-growing app, and where it's proving popular and why. You'll learn about the company behind it, which is challenging Google in its own backyard and wants to do much more than entertain you with diverting videos. All are important to understand TikTok's out-sized impact on the world, and to make your own informed decision as to whether the increasingly heated debate over its impact stems from xenophobic agitprop or well-evidenced concerns about the long-term future of our digital overlords and their government connections.

But beyond that, we'll track what the growth of TikTok really means for us all, for security, privacy and propaganda for the next 25 years or more of our lives. We could be on the cusp of a significant shift in the base of power for almost everything we do online. We're not just talking about which celebrities we idolise and which app we turn to when we're bored. What happens now could shape how we shop, how we bank, and who controls our data – and where it ultimately ends up. It's the reason why a US President tried to stifle TikTok's growth, and why the outcome of that argument – being considered by Joe Biden, the new US President, amid continued frostiness with China – matters quite so much.

On occasion, there will be more questions than answers – simply because TikTok's ascendancy is so new and so stratospheric.

History is happening right before our eyes. But you'll put down this book knowing far more than when you started, and you'll certainly be better equipped to enter the debate.

PART I

THE DREAM OF
A GLOBAL VIDEO APP

1
HAYWIRE
SERVERS

In technology, the first sign of success is failure. Whether it's the runaway popularity of a social media post draining the life from your battery with buzzing notifications of likes and favourites, until you're left staring at a black screen, or the blinking fervour of servers being pushed to their limit, tech has a way of letting you know that you've hit a sweet spot. Unexpected success, in particular, can send the best-laid plans careening off course. Think of it like building a boat: you plan everything around an expected number of passengers, but if too many people jump aboard, the bow cracks and water starts to seep in. Suddenly, you're capsizing.

Alex Zhu, a free-thinking civil engineering graduate from Zheijiang University, one of China's best known technical universities, certainly knew he had a runaway success on his hands when he woke up on 22 July 2016 in Shanghai, China. Zhu, then 35, had worked on Cisco's WebEx conference calling system and SAP's business software in the 2000s and 2010s. He and his 35-year-old colleague Louis Yang had co-founded a lip syncing app, Musical.ly. It allowed people to record 15-second snippets miming along to pop songs and had become a sensation among teenagers. Seven in 10 users had real world friends on the app, and were convincing more and more of their close contacts to try it out. Half of an average user's followers were people they were close to in real life, which meant they were more likely to keep logging onto the app to see what their friends were up to.

When we spoke via a crackly Skype connection that day, he had been roused by a phone call from the app's United States office relaying that its servers had crashed – again. Far from being one of China's stiff-suited apparatchiks, Zhu has always classed himself as a creative type. He defines his job as a 'designtrepeneur'; his social media accounts eschew the formality of using his name, but instead flighty phrases like 'keepsilence' and 'mylonelyhouse.' He laughed when I asked whether Musical.ly had encountered problems because it was too popular. He explained that the amount of web traffic being sent by its 11 million daily active was overwhelming both the company's infrastructure in data centres around the world and the backup it had cobbled together to handle excess traffic.

In fact, an army of 100 million users had been unwittingly overwhelming its servers for six months. When Zhu and Yang first conceived of Musical.ly, they didn't contemplate such rapid growth. 'When the app was initially built, we didn't build it for scalability,' Zhu told me. Befitting his character, he didn't seem too bothered about the data 'issues.'

Even so, everyone working on Musical.ly knew they had to fix problems whenever they arose. App users can be fickle beings. If they can't log in to the app for several hours because of a server outage, they may never return. The popularity of the app in the West meant many of the issues surfaced in the middle of the night in China. Few people knew about the sleepless nights over mis-firing servers, and the general irascibility of engineering teams working on too much stress and too little sleep. 'The team haven't had enough rest,' Zhu said.

While frantically trying to bail out the servers sinking under the weight of too many passengers, Musical.ly's engineering team was also trying to rebuild the way the app communicated with its data centres to prevent it breaching capacity. That was impor-tant because Zhu, speaking on that July morning, had big plans. Musical.ly, which until then had been known as a way for bored teenagers to while away their time doing the digital equivalent of singing into a hairbrush in front of a mirror, was going to change. 'In addition to music, we're using more cultural forms,' said Zhu. He envisaged a future for Musical.ly where users could perform comedy skits to their smartphone camera and share them; could record their own voice and act out scenes; could do silly dances to their favourite songs. 'As long as it's a video format, we think we can do it,' he said. 'The fundamental thinking behind this is that it's every kind of video format for self-expression and social communication.' It was a prescient decision that allowed Musical.ly to build up a massive userbase.

Musical.ly would eventually become TikTok – which has been downloaded by 2.6 billion people worldwide.

TikTok is extraordinarily easy to use. Users pick up a phone, press record, and film a video less than 15 or 60 seconds long using a variety of filters available at the swipe of a finger. They can add a short snippet of music – taken from chart-topping hits, or indeed anywhere – and upload the resulting footage to the app. Then users tag it with hashtags so it can get discovered. As to what is in the video, it's up to users. Parkour artists make death-defying leaps across tall buildings; teenagers in their bedroom dance on the spot and point to political messages they want to make that appear as on-screen captions in front of them. Some people sing. Some people dance. Some people stare. It's frictionless and simple, intuitive and addictive. And even more than YouTube, it demolishes the line between viewer and creator.

TikTok has blown away all records in its short life. In January 2018, TikTok had 54 million monthly active users. By the end of the year, it had 271 million, and the year after that, 507 million. By July 2020, 689 million people – twice as many as Twitter, which was founded in 2006 – logged on every month. In the second quarter of 2020, 50 million people in Europe and 25 million in the United States downloaded TikTok onto their devices. Fifty million Americans open up the app every day – a tenfold rise since January 2018, according to official data from the app itself.

These are the kind of numbers American tech giants can only dream about. YouTube attained two billion monthly active users after 15 years of existence, and Facebook took 13 years. If TikTok keeps its current trajectory, it will probably reach that level in a quarter of the time. The acceleration of technology adoption, with word spreading faster about the hottest new apps, partly explains this growth. But a large part is TikTok engineering its own success by standing out from the crowd.

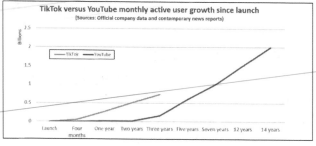

TikTok's growth is outpacing YouTube's

With the benefit of hindsight, it's clear that Zhu, on that crisp summer morning, dared to dream. I had asked him whether he was muscling in on YouTube, which had one billion users at the time, and two other apps, Periscope for livestreaming and Vine for short-form video. Nonchalantly, he replied that he thought Musical.ly had been competing with all three apps for a long time. He was overjoyed with its userbase and demographics: 75% of Musical.ly's users then were women, and 54% of them were under 24 – the 'best possible userbase you could imagine.' He explained: 'They have time, they're creative, and they're social media addicts.' The majority of the users were teenagers, with the most active users between the age of 13 and 20, the average age inching up every month – the result of teenagers and children introducing the app to their parents and grandparents, performing music videos with them. This insight would echo through my mind three-and-a-half years later, when I spoke to TikTok's managing director in the UK, about how 2019 was transformative for the app as families gathered around the Christmas tree and performed a TikTok instead of breaking out the Monopoly set.

'Building a community is very similar to running a country,' Zhu said in an interview back in 2016. 'In the early stage, building a community from scratch is like you just discovered a new land. You give it a new name, and if you want to build an economy you want to build population and you want people to migrate to your country.'

At the time, other countries were much more popular. Zhu singled out Instagram and Facebook, where the economy was very developed. On Musical.ly, there was no population and no economy. So how could he attract people? Zhu, who has long looked outward to the rest of the world, drew on an age-old idea: the promise of the American Dream.

In the old countries of Facebook and Instagram, the social class was already entrenched, and there was little chance of progression for the average person. It's an issue YouTube has long struggled with: research shows that 96.5% of those posting videos on the Google-owned video sharing platform won't make enough money from advertising revenue against their videos alone to reach the poverty line. 'They have almost zero opportunity to go up in the social class,' as Zhu explained.

But in a new land, you can run a centralised economy – channelling most wealth to a small percentage of the population, to enrich those people first. They then become role models, showing that the grass is greener on the other side, encouraging more people to migrate from other apps to Musical.ly. It's a model that continued through to TikTok.

However, at some point the wealth must trickle down. 'Having an American Dream is good, but if it's only a dream, people will wake up eventually.' That also extends to the upper classes and the founding fathers and mothers of a new app economy too. Fame alone is enough to get people to embrace a new platform, certainly – but at some point, they'll wonder where the money is coming from. 'Once they have the fame, it's not enough,' says Zhu. 'They have to monetise.'

Zhu's dream was surprisingly clear, even at that early stage. He had just launched an adjunct app, Live.ly, which combined multiple communication platforms into one single app. It would help Musical.ly break out of the lip syncing niche, and into more general videos. He and Yang were targeting not just the United States and Europe, but south-east Asia, India, Japan and Brazil. Allowing users, who were then called 'musers,' to make different types of videos would also help attract older audiences. Zhu didn't just want the young kids aged 13 to 20. He wanted people in their 20s and 30s.

He had a sense of direction, a boldness of vision, and a commitment to testing. 'We have to do a lot of experiments to see how it goes,' he told me. 'It's too early to predict how big it can be.'

2
THE CONVENTION
CENTRE, 2019

It is February 2019 at VidCon London. This is the first foray into the United Kingdom by the world's biggest online video conference. VidCon connects the two disparate halves of the online video world. For the first day of the event in London, earnest digital marketers in smart suits discuss how to target key demographics, while growth hackers – invariably middle-aged men with bad haircuts and a paunch barely hidden by a branded T-shirt – give away the secrets of how to make it big on YouTube.

Then for the weekend, things get weird. The cavernous halls of the venue clamour with the screams of schoolgirls meeting their idols, and you're as likely to see someone with an LGBTQ+ flag draped over their shoulders and knotted against their clavicle as you are a tailored suit. It's a collision of the corporate and cultural worlds of online video.

It's 10 years since the YouTubers Hank and John Green established VidCon. During that time its rise has mirrored that of YouTube, which transformed itself from an odd site for uploading home videos to something vastly bigger. While a lot of things at

VidCon change, from the number of panels and attendees to the way that ordinary punters are increasingly kept away from the digital video stars turned celebrities, one remains the same: this is primarily a conference about YouTube.

So I am nonplussed at first when a friend, Zoe Glatt, recommends sticking around to watch an upcoming panel. The panel is about a short-form video app I know of but barely use: TikTok. I am not keen. It starts at midday, and I haven't eaten for hours, having chaired an early morning session on YouTubers' mental health.

I know that TikTok is a big thing to people elsewhere, but my knowledge is refracted through layers of distance. So I know that TikTok is popular, but only in the way that people outside the US know that the NFL pays astronomical salaries without ever getting a grip on it, or comprehending why anyone would care about it. But Zoe is persistent, and I could do with sitting in a quiet space away from the hubbub of the conference floor. So I sit in on the TikTok panel.

And everything changes.

Many of the panels held on VidCon's smaller stages are insipid occasions, where creators, managers, advertisers and brand people on the podium talk shop, while audience members languidly scroll through emails on their phone.

The TikTok experience is different. For a start, barring the parents accompanying their children, at 29 I am one of the oldest there – by some distance. The audience members have their hair in braids, and their faces painted with glittery streaks across their cheekbones. They stamp their feet with excitement, and nearly squeal with anticipation. The tenor and tone of the conversation is different. While the panellists talk about business and brand deals and opportunities for the platform to grow, when the moderator opens up the discussion for questions from the floor, over-excited hands stretch up to the sky. Some children teeter on the edge of their seats in order to try and elongate their fingers that extra half-inch.

The questions are as revealing as the diorama I see before me: while most YouTube panels discuss clicks per mille, or CPMs (a mechanism for making money, which is the amount of money a company has to pay to get 1,000 views of its ad) or the benefits of diversifying your income streams, the toughest line of questioning at the TikTok session comes from a cherubic child who asks her idols what they do if they laugh mid-way through recording a video. For the record, the TikTokkers – including Vicky Banham, Hannah Snow, and Laura Edwards – don't really say.

Five months later, the American version of VidCon takes place at the Anaheim Convention Centre in California. It is bigger, bolder and brasher than the UK event. While I am not in attendance, many of my journalistic peers are – and go through the same Damascene revelation I have in February. For them, it is hard to avoid: massed groups of teens throng around shiny-haired, clean-skinned, impeccably tanned and styled youngsters as they dance along in carefully choreographed routines – the raw basis of a TikTok video. Suddenly, TikTok is on the tip of everyone's tongue.

Lil Nas X's record-breaking success at the top of the Billboard charts is largely due to the use of *Old Town Road* as a trope in TikTok videos. Beyonce references TikTok in a song. Even Will Smith joins TikTok. (He joins YouTube in January 2018 and Instagram in December 2017. He eventually signs up for his TikTok account in October 2019.)

But as well as which celebrity is the latest to appear, analysis of the app begins to alter. The conversations around TikTok have changed from simply trying to understand why it is so popular, to something deeper. Could it be an instrument of the Chinese state, burrowing into our collective consciousness for nefarious reasons? Or are the politicians, like the parents, just struggling to understand something so alien to them?

3
THE FIRST GLOBAL CHINESE PLATFORM

More than YouTube or any other video-based social media platform, TikTok is international in its outlook. It's used and loved across the globe, and is China's first real tech success – which has caused headaches and opportunities.

While all the other major technology giants – the Facebooks, Twitters and YouTubes of the world – have emanated from Silicon Valley, TikTok is different. Its history – including through Musical.ly – is deeply rooted in China. And that connection to China makes some people uncomfortable.

For a long time, China was just a factory for American technology companies, a place where cheap components were manufactured and assembled and then loaded into shipping containers for sale to Western consumers half a world away. But in recent years that's shifted. Not just content with making the world's hardware, China has started exporting software. 'Made in China,' where goods designed elsewhere would be put together in the Far East to take advantage of cheap labour, is mutating into 'Created in China': where ideas are born, and then spread to the West. The most high profile of these global innovations is TikTok.

That tie to China causes great unease to geopolitical hawks in the US and Europe, who are wary of the imposition of Chinese apps and services on the Western world. They worry that it's an attempt by the Chinese state to exercise soft power, and to enter our lives. Quirky videos and hashtag challenges will superficially charm their way in through the front door, the thinking goes, before the coding below builds up a granular picture of how each of us lives and works – allowing propaganda and disinformation to be targeted at individuals. The concern is amplified by the growing distrust of all technology, fuelled by the Cambridge Analytica scandal, where a vast amount of personal data about Facebook users was siphoned off for unjustified use in election campaigns worldwide. Post-Cambridge Analytica in 2018, we're more aware than ever of the value of our social media data, and the power companies or individuals wield when they can access it. And while TikTok doesn't require users to set up an account to start exploring its videos, it does need to be accessed through a device – whether your phone via its app, or an internet browser on your tablet, laptop or desktop. And it does generate data.

Various people are trying to figure out what happens to that data. A Californian college student sued TikTok in December 2019, alleging the app transported her data to Chinese servers – something the app vehemently denied. Instead, American users' data is stored at a data centre in Virginia, with a backup kept in Singapore. The fear behind the Chinese connection is that once the data is stored on Chinese territory, the ruling Communist Party can then access it, discerning information about our lives and habits that could be used against us in the future.

For those who think TikTok is nothing but a diversion for teenage users, it's a classic case of alarm, buoyed by a new Cold

War mentality. While there are many concerns about TikTok, the idea that it can see into a teenager's bedroom isn't high on the list – not least when Chinese spies, should they wish, can likely access the exact same images and video by logging onto the same person's social media accounts on American-owned Instagram, Facebook, Snapchat or YouTube. For the sceptics who don't believe TikTok is a deep state plot, there's plenty of evidence to point to that TikTok is an unwitting victim of a misplaced anger at social media in general.

The Cambridge Analytica scandal sent shockwaves through the world, reconfiguring our approach and attitudes to big tech. While previously many had seen social media platforms as benign, helpful enablers of our rapid, interconnected lives, post-Cambridge Analytica we began to appreciate the saying that when you get something for free, you are the product. Our lives were for sale

In the years since, we've seen similar worries about big tech's ability to radicalise our most vulnerable members of society, to poison and sexualise our children, and to continue making money while making us addicted. They have felt able to confront governments head on – for a short time in 2021, Facebook shut down news services to its 17 million Australian users in protest at a proposed law that would have forced it and Google to pay for content.

Whether TikTok is any different from the US-based tech giants in how it handles our data, or targets our interests based on our app usage, is very much still up for question. Despite years of trying, journalists haven't yet come up with evidence of the red phone connecting its owners directly to Xi Jinping, China's president, whose bidding the app is sometimes alleged to do.

And yet the fears still persist. Why?

The story of the internet, and the platforms and websites that live off it, has long been a Western one, with the focus of the microscope centred over Silicon Valley. It's been that way since Bill Gates and Steve Jobs were locked in a tussle for dominance over the square foot of our desks that would house our first home computer, and has continued through the rise of Google, Amazon, Facebook and Apple in the early 21st Century. But things are changing, and not just online. The rise of Chinese companies in the internet space echoes broader societal and economic shifts. China has been rising for decades.

The Committee on Foreign Investment in the United States opened an investigation into TikTok and its Chinese owner in November 2019. The investigation was drummed up in part by fears raised by Senate minority leader Chuck Schumer, a Democrat, and two Republican senators, Tom Cotton and Marco Rubio. In a letter to the US Treasury secretary, Steven Mnuchin, Rubio warned: 'The Chinese government's nefarious efforts to censor information inside free societies around the world cannot be accepted and pose serious long-term challenges to the U.S. and our allies.'

The concerns are obvious, and understandable. While politicians can bring the chief executives of American tech firms to heel through domestic legislation that compels them to turn up to governmental hearings and reform their core operations, directing executives of global companies headquartered outside their jurisdiction is more difficult. It's the first time that's happened in the history of big tech, and it's evidently disliked by some of the most hawkish politicians, whose attitudes to China are mostly negative.

'We understand why people ask questions when the company grows up in China,' Rich Waterworth, TikTok's managing director for the UK and Europe, told me in August 2020. 'We understand the geopolitical situation that leads people to ask those questions, and we get that. We think that's fine.' The questions, says Waterworth, allows TikTok to explain its transparency and openness and quell concerns. Waterworth, a former Google executive, said he has never had concerns about the company's Chinese past, before or since joining the company a year previously.

Some of the fears initially seem well-founded, however. Scroll through TikTok and search for content about Hong Kong, which China considers part of its territory rather than a sovereign state, and which was subject to significant, long-lasting street protests calling for independence throughout 2019 and early 2020, and you'll encounter very little content. The *Guardian* uncovered guidelines given to content moderators working to remove questionable or unsuitable material from TikTok, which seemed to indicate that the app did not allow content 'inciting the independence' of Tibet and Taiwan, as well as that of Northern Ireland and the Republic of Chechnya. Censored too were politically sensitive subjects in China, such as videos about the 1989 Tiananmen Square protests in Beijing. TikTok's further content moderation guidelines, revealed by a German publication, ban all political content – which just happens to include many issues the Chinese state finds so troublesome to air in public. TikTok itself said there was nothing sinister about the guidelines: 'We have never been asked by the Chinese government to remove any content and we would not do so if asked. Period,' it said. 'We are not influenced by any foreign government, including the Chinese government; TikTok does not operate in China, nor do we have any intention of doing so in the future.' These are all 'facts,' says Waterworth. 'We've tried to be very explicit and clear about it, but no data is shared or given to the Chinese government and we wouldn't give it to them if asked.'

We'll look in more detail at data later.

4
CHINA VERSUS
THE WORLD

The gatherings of the National Propaganda and Ideology Work
Conference in Beijing aren't a highlight of anyone's year. Yet
its 2013 edition, held in the Chinese capital in August, was instructive for those wanting to know the reason for concern about the
rise of TikTok in the West.

At the conference, Xi Jinping, China's newly-installed president
and a longtime Communist Party apparatchik, made a speech on
China's ideology. Couched within that speech – languorous, long
and meandering – was an interesting passage on how Xi saw the
future of China's internet. 'Western anti-China forces have constantly and vainly tried to exploit the internet to topple China,'
Xi told his audience. 'Whether we can stand our ground and win
this battle over the internet has a direct bearing on our country's
ideological and political security.'

For China, control over its internet is vital to its national security. As Wang Yongzhang, who was once the director of China's
Cultural Industries Division in its Ministry of Culture, explains
it, culture is the 'thorniest question' for Chinese censors while

it's the 'least problematic' idea for Westerners. Culture is about innovation and free expression: it's about mirroring society, and shifting conversations. All of those things are a given in the West, but challenge China's rulers.

A precarious and repressive regime that is known by the rest of the world to have conducted human rights abuses, the Chinese Communist Party maintains its unsteady grip on power by ensuring what is said in cyberspace follows its line. That's done by the world's most intrusive digital monitoring and policing regime. (Famously, you can't mention Winnie the Pooh on social platforms like Weibo, China's version of Twitter, because it's a mocking phrase used by rebellious anti-governmental campaigners who think the cartoon character bears a resemblance to Xi.) China is encircled by the Great Firewall – and though it's porous and able to be circumvented with a virtual private network, or VPN, that acts as a way of hiding your digital tracks – it's still powerful. 'The boundary between reality and virtuality is becoming more ambiguous,' China's cyberspace administration wrote in 2017. 'Cybersecurity is not only related to the security of our country and society, but more importantly, is related to the personal interests of every netizen.'

China has had total control over its internet since its then premier, Li Peng, passed State Council Order 195 in February 1996. The order, laughably called 'temporary regulations governing computer information networks and the internet,' was strengthened by the Ministry of Public Security a year later when the rules were meant to run out.

Almost all internet traffic into and out of China passes through three exchanges in Beijing, Shanghai and Guangzhou, where any infelicitous material can be sifted out from public consumption.

Not that that needs to happen in most instances. Services and apps that operate in China know the rules of the road, and tend to follow them, often bending their will to that of the regime.

Through these levers China has managed to achieve what in 2000 Bill Clinton equated to nailing jelly to the wall: a relatively docile digital sphere. Most people and companies self-censor, and those that don't are often caught. Western companies coming into China have to follow the same rules, adopting policies that they outwardly call adapting to cultural norms but most people would plainly call censorship. Chinese internet users can visit LinkedIn, though the experience isn't quite as it is in the West. Yahoo launched a Chinese subsidiary in 1999; Google followed it a year later, though then left, ostensibly because it disliked censoring its content. It's recently been considering a return through a project internally codenamed Dragonfly.

All companies operating in China have to be willing to give up their data on request to the authorities. That has people in the West concerned that would also be the case for the Chinese-owned TikTok. Reputable cybersecurity experts have pored through TikTok's code and found that it doesn't include some of the things people worry the most about, suggesting that a Western user's data is unlikely to end up on the computer screen of a Chinese spy sat in Beijing, at least not through conventional means.

But it gives people pause for thought – and quite rightly so. Not for nothing has Xi Jinping repeatedly exhorted his people to 'Tell good stories about China to the world.' TikTok is one of those good stories: a Chinese-born app that is now a cultural powerhouse. To a Western world, used to dealing in absolutes, there's no way to separate China's authoritarian control over digital firms operating within its borders from its lack of control over everything that company does. Anyone who slots into that system and signs up to follow its principles in theory must also be doing so in practice.

Yet those within the system often work on a more pragmatic approach. They pay lip service to the rules, and are able to differentiate working under one system and another. I see it personally in the Chinese journalism students I teach at a Western university. They discuss things they would never dream of doing so back in China because they know the system they are under gives them the right to speak freely, unlike back at home. They understand the rules, and are able to hold two moral frameworks in their heads at once.

In trying to stop an outward looking, cosmopolitan Chinese app from gaining traction in the West, there is a risk that we dull innovation. Competition has spurred on the massive developments in the digital world. It's what allowed the companies we interact with every day to thrive. If the West bans some market participants just because it doesn't like where they originate and fear that they are fostering their cultural norms and practices, effective competition will be reduced and the internet Balkanised: a fragmented, unequal place shorn of all the things that have made it great.

It also is a strange turn of events for an app that was forged in the market, strengthened through acquisition and capitalist competition, and run by a far-seeing Chinese entrepreneur who studied Western businessmen.

CREATOR FOCUS
LUCA GALLONE

Name: Luca Gallone
Username: @lucagallone
Following: 71
Followers: 9.6M
Likes: 159.7M
Speciality: Sleight of hand, up-close magic

Luca Gallone found the reach of TikTok when he was performing a private magic show in the Maldives. Gallone had started meandering around tables at weddings aged 16, doing tricks to perk up guests between speeches. An appearance on *Britain's Got Talent* in 2015 wowed all four judges, leading to more live work, where he specialises in sleight of hand and up-close magic – which goes down well at parties and in short videos. By the start of 2020 Gallone had 6.7 million followers on TikTok. But the booking in the Maldives, 5,400 miles from his home in the UK, hadn't come from his online fame – and yet TikTok kept intruding on him here.

The 25-year-old had ducked into a small shop to pick up a bite to eat – a chocolate bar or something similar – and felt the eyes of the shopkeeper on him. He didn't know whether the store owner thought he was trying to steal from the shelves, but the gaze lingered a little longer than was comfortable.

Gallone continued with his shopping and walked up to the counter. As he did, the inquisitive look continued, and the shopkeeper turned his phone to Gallone. On the screen was one of Gallone's biggest viral hits on TikTok – a video where he slaps a straw against his palm twice while sitting next to a customer at a branch of McDonald's, before depositing the straw behind his ear before the third slap so a friend can put it around the mark's shoulder and into his soft drink, an illusion that provokes wide-eyed wonder.

'He shows me this video – the straw video, and asks: "Is this you?",' says Gallone.

The shopkeeper was one of millions to watch the video on TikTok – 116 million since it was posted in April 2019, with millions more encountering it through reposts on other social media. When Gallone reposted it as a throwback, it gained another 45 million eyeballs. 'Those kinds of numbers, you can't get on another app,' he says. 'It's really crazy.'

He's seen the full transition of TikTok from a lip syncing lark to a media titan, with a diverse range of content providing hours of entertainment. 'The rate at which I've seen the app grow is absolutely phenomenal,' Gallone said. He has experienced a massive increase in audiences. When he first started posting, he'd be overjoyed with a million views on a single video, when now he can get hundreds of times that number.

Alongside Alt TikTok, where anonymous teenagers perform oddball skits, to LGBTQ TikTok, cooking TikTok and witchtok, magic TikTok is a huge yet discrete part of the app. Tricks are well-suited to TikTok: the editing options and sleight of hand make for impressive videos, while the cadence of an individual trick – set-up, peril and punchline – almost exactly mirror the guidance TikTok gives to creators for how to create dopamine-inducing content.

Gallone praises the way TikTok makes it easy for people to transform from passive viewers to active creators. 'When you start, it's a little bit daunting going on to, say, YouTube,' explains Gallone. 'You've got to edit, and you think you've got to have a really flash camera.' Yet on

TikTok, most of the editing tools you'll need are contained within the app. You can also filter your videos to give them a professional gloss. The most expensive outlay the average TikToker needs is a ring light (a halo of lighting on a tripod) that gives your skin the right kind of glow. One costs about $20.

The comparatively low barrier to entry 'opens the door for everyone to get started,' says Gallone. 'That's really helped a lot of people get on there, and will start the careers of a lot of really amazing future influencers and social media stars.'

PART II

WELCOME TO BYTEDANCE

5
THE SUPER
APP STORE

Ask most people what ByteDance is and they'll likely meet you with a blank stare. Yet it is the owner of TikTok and a host of other world-leading apps. Founded in March 2012, it's worth about $180 billion – up from its $75 billion in 2018 when the Japanese technology investors SoftBank Group bought into the company. Despite the fact that its apps are used by two billion people worldwide, earning it $34 billion in revenue in 2020, ByteDance deliberately keeps a low profile among the general public in the West. It wants its products to take centre stage.

It's a strategy devised by its low-key, but intensely-driven founder, Yiming Zhang. Whereas his fellow Chinese rival, Musical.ly's Alex Zhu, is creative and flighty, Zhang is measured and focussed. Compared to his more brash counterparts in China, such as Jack Ma, the former boss of Alibaba Group, who's known for his exuberance and outgoing personality, he is even a little dull. Considered. He practises 'delayed gratification.' He's rational – though his choice of clothing, T-shirts and jeans, makes him more laid back than the average Chinese executive. Imagine the slightly underwhelming disappointment of Mark Zuckerberg, rather than the zany pinball personality of Elon Musk.

Born in 1983 in the city of Longyan in the coastal province of Fujian that's known for having the highest proportion of emigrants to the Western world in all of China, Zhang is, however, fiercely independent. While many people entering China's tech sector are comfortable to land a job at one of the pre-existing Chinese tech giants, Zhang ignored that route. He was not after the quick buzz of instant success by piggybacking onto a pre-existing victor: he played the long game.

He studied software engineering at Tianjin's Nankai University, after his preferred subject, biology, was oversubscribed, and he didn't like his initial modules on microelectronics. He was a studious learner, but also enjoyed the social aspect of higher education. As well as his wife, he met many of his closest friends on campus and at barbecues he hosted after hours. While most university students would spend their years partying as much as studying, Zhang didn't. That's partly because Nankai, based in Tianjin, a port city in the north of the country, wasn't as bustling as Beijing. But it's also a measure of the man. In his first two years at university, he devoured books, including biographies of Steve Jobs, and Jack Welch's treatise on business, *Winning*. By reading about the businessmen and women he idolised, Zhang became more patient about choosing his career and plotting out his progression. 'You see that a lot of great people led pretty nondescript lives when they were younger, and their success is gradual,' he told students at his former university. 'Everyone starts off being an ordinary person.'

In 2011, Zhang was in his sixth year after graduating. He had bumped around a number of Chinese tech startups, including a popular travel website called Kuxun and one called Fanfou, and even spent time working for Microsoft – an experience he apparently didn't enjoy because of the stringent corporate thinking and strong oversight that was commonplace throughout the firm. Frustrated, he set up a company of his own, called 99Fang, a property search engine.

It was on a commute on the Beijing metro network that Zhang came across the idea for another app – Toutiao. Like the books he had devoured while at university, Zhang also read newspapers and magazines cover-to-cover. 'At the time, I felt that the transmission of information was a very big deal,' he told students at another Chinese university in 2018. 'Differences in the efficiency of how information is transmitted could lead to very large differences in the efficiency of and cooperation across all of society, as well as in individual cognitions.'

As newspapers started to wither, Zhang realised there were other ways people were getting their news. 'I noticed that fewer and fewer people were reading newspapers on subways,' he told students at his old university. He looked at smartphone sales figures, and noticed they had boomed during 2011. He put two and two together. 'I thought smartphones would replace newspapers to become the most important medium of information distribution.'

More intuitively, Zhang saw the future would be powered by artificial intelligence (AI) – which remains at the core of every ByteDance app and service today. He imagined a future where people were served news headlines based on their interests, rather than who paid the most for advertising, or what editors of print newspapers thought was worth reading that day. He wanted to 'connect people with information.' It didn't matter that, although he knew software engineering, he didn't have the slightest clue how to develop an AI system. He would learn. And his friends from university, who he'd have over for barbecues, could help. Zhang hired a businessman to take over the day-to-day operations of 99Fang, and devoted his time to developing other apps.

That was because Zhang, ever studious and always paying attention, had noticed a massive opportunity in the market – or at least, that's what he recounted with the benefit of hindsight. He had got his hands on the first iPhone soon after its release in 2007, and was amazed by having a supercomputer in his pocket. When working on 99Fang and other companies before launching ByteDance, he saw the rise of mobile internet slowly stirring. By the end of 2011, he had decided to make the leap and to start a new company. 'This has something to do with reading biographies,' he said. 'In the face of big trends, people are often oblivious and don't feel anything until afterwards. In 2011, I really felt that the progress of science and technology will create a new field. I foresaw that there will be major and profound innovations and profound changes. This change has yet to stop.'

He foresaw a global revolution and wanted to ensure his company was at the centre of it. From the off, ByteDance set out to be as 'borderless as Google.'

ByteDance published an app: Neihan Duanzi. The name translates to something roughly equivalent to 'implied (or innuendo) jokes.' Neihan Duanzi was a simple app where users could share memes. It was a cross between Imgur, the image hosting website, home to lots of funny images and GIFs, and Reddit, where many of those images are shared.

Neihan Duanzi was hugely popular, quickly growing to 200 million users at its peak. These people weren't just casual users, either. In the true tradition of the odder corners of the internet, they were some of the most committed posters. They created and bought merchandise celebrating their connection to the app. They met up in parking lots to build up more of a community, and took photographs to celebrate their oddity. They had a slightly subversive anthem of their own called 'On Earth' that they would use to identify fellow users. They'd sometimes even honk coded messages using car horns while parked at red lights to see if there was anyone else with a slightly twisted mind and a love of humour nearby. The honking got so loud and commonplace that several cities issued orders banning the use of car horns.

ByteDance also developed its news app, Toutiao ('headlines'), which presented users with a personally tailored newspaper's-worth of stories every time they opened it. Its data demands were enormous: identifying what a user wants and sifting through reams of information and news stories to provide it to them is hugely resource-intensive. By 2017, hundreds of engineers were working in a building called the Toutiao Dwarf Building in Beijing. They coded and tinkered on open-plan desks lined up around a central, glass cylinder that operated as the company's main meeting room. Staff were driven to develop apps that grew faster than others. One engineer, who left Baidu, China's Google, for ByteDance, said their work ethics were as different as day and night. A strident, young company coming on in leaps and bounds, Toutiao and the firm in general grew continuously. The employee compares it to being in on the ground floor of Facebook in its chaotic, anarchic earliest days (and believes ByteDance will become as big and as respected as Mark Zuckerberg's company, and play as important a role in our lives as Facebook does now).

In 2018, ByteDance vice president Yang Zhenyuan said that Toutiao used up more than 1,500 petabytes, or 1.5 billion gigabytes, of data storage. And the amount of data processed every single day was 50 petabytes, the equivalent of streaming nearly 11 million two-hour long HD movies on Netflix. Not all of that was Toutiao's own content, though. The app was criticised in its early days for aggregating content without permission from news outlets and serving it up within its own app. There were even allegations that adverts that were in original stories for other products were replaced with new ads, sold through Toutiao, from which the app would take a cut. Zhang and ByteDance didn't make many friends through their strategy, but they did pull in the users to Toutiao. Within three months of its launch in August 2012, Toutiao had 10 million of them.

Those users grew in number, and spent more and more time in the app – upwards of an hour every day. And because Zhang recognised the power of AI to make an app 'stickier,' or more engaging and likely to keep people hooked, each interaction they had within the app was tracked and used to improve the experience the next time. It was a virtuous circle of improvement, using information like how a user swiped through the content, where they tapped, how they stopped and scrolled through articles, depending on the time of day and where they were based, to make Toutiao more engaging.

'After I graduated, whether I was working on a search engine or a social networking site, it was really all about distributing information,' he told students at a meeting at his former university. 'Search engines organised the distribution of information, while social networking sites used people as nodes to organise the flow of information, and recommendation engines use users' interests to more granularly organise the distribution of information,' he said. So core to the development of ByteDance as a company was the creation, recommendation and distribution of information that Zhang took the idea to heart, installing an efficiency engineering department within the company to help improve the flow of communication within the firm.

Zhang knew that AI-powered apps on smartphones were the way of the future. And he had the financial backing to exploit their rise. Investors flocked to invest in ByteDance because of the success of Toutiao. It was an amazing rise for a company founded in a four-bedroom apartment. Ad hoc meetings would be held in the different bedrooms, none more than 10 square metres, ByteDance's earliest employees cramped and crowded around furniture. And within a year of Toutiao's launch, Zhang was already telling people that he thought the AI-powered model could go global. In a presentation to management, the declaration was clear: ByteDance was going to 'attempt commercialisation and internationalisation.' In a four-part plan for the future presented on slide 24 of an uninspiring deck of materials shown in January 2013 to executives, part four was building out an English version of Toutiao to get users in English-speaking countries. At the time competition was hotting up for the attention of phone users. There was an app race for video viewers.

6
THE IMPORTANCE OF MEMES

My friend Fraser helped get me hooked onto YouTube, which transformed into a career as a journalist covering every twist and turn of its journey to become the world's second-most visited website. While teenagers we spent hours sitting in front of a television at our houses, watching whatever YouTube's algorithm suggested. And he's also the person who first got me into Vine.

Vine, a video sharing platform that was TikTok's spiritual forefather, was set up in January 2013, less than a year after Zhang had founded ByteDance. Every video on Vine had to be 6.4 seconds or less. It gave birth to many of online video's biggest stars, and had a longer-lasting effect than its few years as an active app would suggest. Without Vine, we wouldn't have the stars Shawn Mendes, Jake Paul, or Lele Pons – all of them household names to a generation of youngsters. But it was ahead of its time, gaining a notoriety as a springboard to something more, rather than as an end destination for someone who wanted to parlay online fame into a long-lasting career. In that sense, Vine was unlucky: its popularity coincided with an era in which social media wasn't the established entertainment platform. Traditional media snootily dismissed any stars of the small screen then with the moniker 'e-celebrities' or 'social media stars.' This was before YouTubers presented TV shows, sold out stadiums on tours, and topped the music charts. The medium also worked against it. Limited to infinitesimally small video durations, Vine's video stars had only a few options. They could perform hyperspeed comedy skits, or prance and prat around for people's entertainment. They could not connect with their audience on the platform and build up a parasocial relationship: the friend-like bond that separates the new ranks of new media celebrities from the Hollywood film stars who seem so detached from the public.

Vine was also an untrammelled source of creativity. It was riotous. Opening it up felt like being let loose in a madhouse full of gurning faces, outrageous pratfalls, and wacky acting that often veered on the edge of acceptability – and sometimes tip-toed onto the wrong side. People were inventive and creative. They were crazy. Some small memes built up a head of steam and spread within its userbase.

One of them came about because an 11-year-old boy would follow every move of a skateboarding YouTuber. Gregor Reynolds watched every video that Ty Moss put on YouTube. On the day that Vine was published on app stores worldwide, Moss posted his review of Vine on YouTube. Gregor immediately downloaded the app onto his phone and began to mess around with it.

At the time, Gregor's father Stewart had been in the doldrums. His web development business had been hacked. Two months later, a major contract hadn't been renewed, and coupled with the reputational loss and disappearance of regular business, he had been forced to close the firm. 'It was a catastrophic business collapse,' Stewart Reynolds says, looking back with regret. He moped around for a couple of years, by his own admission trying to keep depression and bailiffs at bay. His wife's salary as a school secretary wouldn't pay all the bills. When Gregor told him about this new app, Vine, that he had heard about, Reynolds' first thought wasn't that it would be a ticket to success and riches. He just wanted a reason to laugh every day. He'd spent too many days going to bed, realising he hadn't managed to muster a single smile.

One day, when his wife was at work and his two sons were at school in Canada, Reynolds decided he'd not just watch Vines, but would also make one of his own. He thought he was too old to appear in front of the camera, so he grabbed a 12-inch plastic figurine of the *Star Wars* character Chewbacca he had had since he was 10. He started performing more silly skits on the app. They would be praised by his friends at the pub where he went to drown his sorrows on the weekend.

Under the username Brittlestar, by August 2013 Reynolds had built up a respectable following. But it was one video he made, called 'Put Your Finger on the Screen', that sent him into the social media stratosphere. Standing in front of a red brick wall, the bespectacled, spiky haired father implored viewers to put their finger on the screen and wiggle it up and down. He paused for a second, then cut to a shot of a light switch flicking on and off.

The father posted the video to Vine around 9.20am, just as his children were starting to settle down to school. By the time they were standing in the lunch queue at noon, it had over 100,000 likes. Reynolds' Vine following grew from around 3,500 to more than 100,000. He had hit on a winning formula, and milked it.

The next day, he posted another video with the same conceit. This time, users putting their finger on the screen and wiggling their digit could send a glass of orange squash careening over the edge of a pint glass. It did equally well.

The formula lasted for a week before Reynolds realised he'd need to try something new. He tried another idea, called Summer's Not Over, where he stapled a solitary leaf to a tree in the middle of a winter snowstorm, demanding the tree didn't quit on him and give up to the changing of the seasons. It did well – and gained the attention of Disney, who sent him a private message on Twitter, asking if he would be interested in collaborating.

Soon after, the entire Reynolds family was on a plane to California, paid for by Disney. He did a total of five advertising campaigns for Disney on Vine, and it changed his life. 'We had this catastrophic business collapse, so fiscally, when you go from wondering how to pay the mortgage to having Disney pay you $5,000 for a couple of six-second videos, and to pay for you to go out there and everything, it's life altering,' he says. He met fellow Viners, and was invited to the White House as a guest of Barack Obama as part of a delegation to welcome the Canadian prime minister Justin Trudeau on his first official visit to the US.

Reynolds loved Vine because of its similarity to another format he had spent years devouring: the comics section of the newspaper. Like those cartoons, you knew what you were getting with Vine. There were only ever three or four panels, and there was a set up and pay off to a joke. If you didn't like it, you hadn't invested much time in it. It was something that, in the early- and mid-2010s, was unusual in a world dominated by YouTube. 'Short-form content had never been done, and a whole crop of people learned how to make entertaining content in 6.4 seconds,' says Reynolds.

'You could sit down with Vine for two hours and consume literally hundreds of people's content.'

Vine became a sensation. That made some of its successful creators want more of the fruits of its success – which worried Vine.

7
WE WANT
OUR MONEY

By 2015, two years after its launch, Vine was in trouble, and its owners didn't know what to do. Twitter had bought the company after failing to buy the fast-growing picture-posting site Instagram. Vine had been allowed to operate independently on a separate floor of Twitter's New York office.

Under its new owners Facebook, Instagram had launched a video feature that was eating into Vine's userbase. The number of daily active Vine users – a key measure of popularity – was plunging. The problem was that Vine didn't just keep its creators – the people who made its app what it was – at arm's length. It blatantly ignored them. Its owners were programming people, and they didn't want to engage with the talent the app was developing. In fact, says Karyn Spencer, Vine's head of creator development, there was an outright allergy at Vine to talking about or planning for the ability for creators to make money.

But the situation couldn't continue. Three weeks into her role at Vine, Spencer was brought into an office and told the situation was at a code red. Not only were user numbers falling, but many of Vine's top names, recognising they weren't going to get paid on the platform, were performing in a perfunctory way. They would still upload videos, but it would be to cajole their fans onto other platforms where they could make money through advertising. Spencer was asked to come up with a global talent strategy that would stop the grumbling and keep the creators engaged. It was a hard task – not least because none of the staff at Vine had ever spoken to the Viners they now wanted to win onside. 'What I realised was that while Vine stars had become a very valuable piece of the digital media industry and they had gotten represented by agents and managers and been making all this money on brand deals, when they'd have a glitch with Vine or wanted to speak to someone there, they couldn't,' she says with a laugh. Some of the biggest Viners on the planet – the names and faces that were bringing people to the app in their droves – were left emailing a generic info@vine.co email address.

That caused resentment and anger that Spencer had to puncture, fast. She developed a plan to re-engage with creators at three tiers: the emerging creators who wouldn't be big for another year, but needed support to get there; the mid-level creators who needed massaging and help to become truly big; and the superstar top-level creators who needed bespoke help. One of her first actions in the plan was to throw an event at Venice, California, for Andrew Bachelor, a Canadian comedian known on the app as King Bach, who was Vine's biggest name. The event was to congratulate Bachelor for a clutch of awards he had won in the previous year from industry bodies. 'Everyone had acknowledged King Bach was the top Viner but Vine,' was Spencer's rationale. There was a new regime in town, and things were changing. Creators would get merchandise branded with Vine logos to help them feel engaged; they'd get a partner manager who would be their point of contact for any help they needed.

The plan worked for the emerging creators and the mid-level ones, but the top creators had a sense of entitlement. And they lived together in 1600 Vine, a luxury apartment block in Los Angeles that had become popular with new media celebrities starting to strike it rich on social media, and was as a result becoming something like the 2015 equivalent of *Animal House*. Each fuelled the others' displeasure at the platform. They had become overtly hostile towards Vine, because they believed they were responsible for the app's popularity. They were mad at being ignored, and they wanted to be paid.

Eighteen of these top creators asked Spencer for a meeting and to sign a non-disclosure agreement. 'I spent an hour at least sitting in a conference room with them just listening to all of them yell, basically, about how furious they were to be a part of a platform that never recognised them as being important,' she says. They had come with a game plan: they reckoned if they all collectively left Vine at the same time, they could tank the app's success. They were that confident about their power over the app's impressionable userbase.

They then put forward their demand: be paid $1.2 million to post three Vines a week for a year. Spencer left the meeting battered but elated. She thought 18 of them wanted a collective $1.2 million. She had done the sums, and thought that was a fair price for three videos a week, 52 weeks a year. She reckoned that it secured content for a year from the app's biggest names, and bought Vine time to develop the mid-level creators with whom they hadn't entirely burned their bridges, so even if after 12 months the biggest stars left (which she thought they would), they'd have people to replace them. Spencer could see a sensible way out. She had the support of the leaders at Vine.

Then two things happened. When Vine's leadership reported the result of the meeting and the next steps to Twitter's executive board, there was pushback. Twitter was wary about paying anyone for content, fearing that the demand for money would migrate from Vine to its eponymous, loss-making platform. (Spencer didn't think that would be the case, arguing that Twitter is used for a different purpose.) At the same time, representatives of the 18 biggest stars sent through the paperwork formalising their proposal. They weren't asking for $1.2 million in total. They were asking for $1.2 million each. Twitter didn't want to pay the money. Vine itself was loss-making and was still being bankrolled by Twitter. 'That was a difficult conversation to have with the creators,' says Spencer. The social media celebrities weren't going to get what they asked for.

As the penny dropped – or didn't – the big creators started spreading the word to other creators, with the intention of drumming up more support against the company. But that backfired on them. The community at large wondered why they wanted so much money. Most Viners who received a brand deal were thankful for the little cash they got. They were keen on the platform for its creativity, not its capitalism – and they didn't see why obnoxious teenagers who they thought had lucked out on social media deserved many multiples of the average wage.

In the end, the top creators left. They were already halfway out of the door. Vine closed in large part because of poor leadership, not because it lost its biggest stars. But the loss of those stars – because they weren't being rewarded by the platform they were attracting a large audience to – would be a stark lesson to a shrewd social media entrepreneur who wanted to avoid the mistakes of his predecessors – Yiming Zhang. And there were actually two things to grasp from Vine. First, don't ignore your best-performing creators (they need some money). Secondly, don't let them become too powerful. But before we get to TikTok, we need to tell the story of two other apps that would be folded into the ByteDance family, each of which would lend their key features to the world's smartest short-form video app.

8
ACQUIRING
FAME

ByteDance is a story of ingenuity and astute marshalling of re-sources, pooling the skills and software that's needed across a suite of apps, whether serving up memes, news headlines or short-form, snackable videos, in China or elsewhere. But what people often overlook when they tell the story of TikTok's rise is how much buyouts fuelled its growth. ByteDance has made at least 17 separate purchases over the course of its existence. A number have been purchases of AI companies, such as Jukedeck, a London-based computer-generated music composer, which the company acquired and subsumed into itself in 2019. Coupled with ByteDance's in-house team, such acquisitions enabled the company behind TikTok to expand its technology, and, as a result, grow rapidly across the world.

One of the buyouts was created by John Bolton. At the time he was deflated. The family man readily admits it as we chat on the phone one summer morning in 2020, cars whizzing by in the background as a child occasionally pesters him to play.

Three years earlier in 2017, Bolton was scratching his head. He'd been the fifth person to join a company called Flipagram in April 2014, moving into the company's chi-chi Los Angeles office, and had seen the app – which allowed people to record short videos set to chart-topping music – boom. In under three years, it had been downloaded 300 million times – huge numbers – and went viral over the course of a matter of weeks in 2014. At one point, it was the number one downloaded app in 180 countries worldwide.

Flipagram had raised $70 million from investors, and was one of the buzziest social media sensations of the late 2010s. Suitors had come knocking, and one had done enough to grab the attention of the company's founders. Employees were thrumming with excitement at the prospect of becoming a Google, a Facebook or an Apple 'acqui-hire'.

Little wonder, then, that Bolton and his colleagues were befuddled when they looked at the name linked to Flipagram. ByteDance didn't ring a bell. When he turned to Google to find out more about his new bosses, things didn't get any better. 'I was disappointed,' Bolton readily admits. He'd never heard of ByteDance, and besides, what Chinese tech company had ever been successful outside of China?

For Yiming Zhang, Flipagram was a tempting proposition. It had immensely powerful content creation tools – the kinds of easy access to chart hits and a wide range of filters and stickers to lay on top of video footage that everyday users wanted. But it didn't have a clue how to serve it up to users. People would create their videos in Flipagram, then rather than posting it to the app's own users, they'd save the completed video down, open up another social network and post it there. The app became so popular because every video that was exported bore a watermark explaining it had been made within Flipagram, driving more people to check it out – something that would later help TikTok slip into the public consciousness.

By then, ByteDance had its own powerful recommendation system, honed on the news aggregator Toutiao and finetuned through the company's other apps. It was able to innately understand what people wanted, regardless of what kind of content it was. Each side was missing something the other could provide. It seemed like a perfect fit. The question was a simple one: 'Yiming says, "We have all this technology, you have all this content, what happens if you put it together?", recalls Bolton, who has spent the last three years planning his own startup, Super Hi-Fi, an AI-powered audio platform.

The answer was success. ByteDance bought Flipagram, and Bolton spent a lot more time in Beijing, working for ByteDance. The work ethic was entirely different from Los Angeles: when he arrived in the office every morning at 8am, Bolton would often find people sleeping at their desks. But the people shared a global outlook and an Americanised culture that stemmed from the boss himself. 'Yiming was very kind, polite and respectful,' says Bolton. He was bookish, a poindexter, with a buzzcut and a gentle demeanour. Bolton knew all about the music industry, having brokered agreements with record labels for Flipagram, and was brought in to do the same for ByteDance. 'I had information, knowledge and experience they didn't have, and they wanted to learn,' he says.

9
ALEX ZHU

The second app to make TikTok what it is today was one we've already met – Musical.ly. Just as Yiming Zhang came up with the idea to launch ByteDance's first real success, Toutiao, when he was sitting on the subway and noticed that a scroll through a smartphone was beginning to replace an unfurled newspaper, Alex Zhu had the idea for Musical.ly while riding the train in Mountain View, California. Zhu watched how the teenaged passengers clowned about for selfies and videos. Zhu had worked for a number of business-focused tech companies. In 2013, he teamed up with a friend, Louis Yang, to set up a new company, Cicada Education. It was designed to help people – predominately teenagers – learn new ideas or subjects by watching short, sub-five-minute videos produced by experts. Zhu and Yang coaxed $250,000 out of China Rock Capital Management to bankroll the company. They spent 92% of the money developing the platform, connecting with relevant experts in their fields, and producing videos. On the day they released the app, Zhu says he knew it would tank. The experts struggled to distil their knowledge, built up over the course of years of experience, into short videos. And the videos themselves weren't engaging enough. The experts had difficulty producing them; they were a hodge-podge of amateurish content that undersold the expertise on offer. 'It was doomed to be a failure,' he said.

Six months into their project there was $20,000 left in the slush fund Zhu and Yang had obtained from Chinese investors. They decided to scrap the idea of the educational video platform and do something Zhu reckoned his teenaged audience wanted, based on the way he watched them goof about on the train in California. He set the small team he had hired for Cicada a new job: to develop an app that tech-literate teens wouldn't be able to put down. One that would allow them to create the sort of short videos that Cicada had been trying to do, but couldn't successfully. Zhu knew that the barrier to entry for making compelling videos had to be lower than it was when he just left the experts he hired for Cicada to their own devices. 'If you want to do a content-based community, the content and creation has to be extremely light,' he said. 'Something that you can finish within a few seconds, not minutes or hours.' He also knew that teenagers liked lip syncing to their favourite songs, and would overlay them with brash stickers and wild effects. Within a month they had produced Musical.ly.

Released on app stores in July 2014, around 500 people a day started downloading it. Crucially, once they opened the app and started using it, they kept returning – a battle few apps win. The founders had struck it lucky. They hit upon a subculture that was growing. As well as similar apps like Triller and Dubsmash, there was a TV programme called *Lip Sync Battle* that had gained a cult following in the United States. The Thursday night broadcasts of *Lip Sync Battle* would result in a weekly spike in downloads for Musical.ly, as people typed in 'lip sync' into their app store search bars and came across the app. Zhu and his team also gamed the app store system, recognising that it prioritised the app name above the keywords that would appear in search results – and better still, allowed very long app names. So they inserted all the keywords people might search for to find their app in the product's name, benefiting from that traffic. The app cycled through names like 'Musical.ly: make awesome music videos with all kinds of effects for Instagram and Facebook Messenger.' Downloads kept coming.

When I spoke to Zhu in the middle of 2016, it took weeks of emails and one entirely missed appointment to get him on Skype. The reasons he gave were sensible and justifiable – the melting servers struggling under the weight of Musical.ly's popularity, and the imminent launch of Live.ly, which would allow big name 'musers' to make big money from their livestreams. A few months after launching Live.ly in 2016, Musical.ly said that its top 10 live streamers had earned an average of $46,000 over two weeks from donations by their fans.

At Flipagram, a rival before it was taken over, there was concern at how much savvier Musical.y was. 'We realised they had evolved our use case into something much more engaging and entertaining,' John Bolton says. 'They formed an engagement loop, or a fame loop, where kids were getting onto Musical.ly not to necessarily share moments with friends, but to try and get "famous." And people were getting famous. We didn't have that dynamic on our service.'

Zhu knew exactly what a commercial success he had created with Musical.ly, despite being a carefree spirit. (He was even willing to poke fun at China's restrictive politics in a November 2016 interview at a technology conference, saying that Chinese people were so interested in the US presidential debates going on at the time because they had none of their own.) He surveyed early users about their thoughts on the app, enacting the advice they offered. The so-called 'participatory design' was a crucial part of Musical.ly's early growth, involving hundreds of users on WeChat, a Chinese messenger platform, with whom they had daily conversations about the app – as well as life, and what they felt was important. Those users were generally young teenagers – the type that Zhu had told me were a core component of Musical.ly's user-base. They also talked to their peers at school, and advocated for others to download the app.

But Zhu was very unlike the even more focussed Yiming Zhang. While Zhu talked to me about the runaway success of Musical.ly, the blown-out servers and his dreams of the future from Musical.ly's office in Shanghai, 1,200 kilometres north in Beijing, Zhang was partway through a 200-day race to develop a video app of his own.

10
AN EASY BIRTH

ByteDance was riding high: Chinese people were regularly opening Toutiao. So in 2016, ByteDance decided to see if it could adapt the immense algorithmic power it had accumulated by monitoring how Chinese people viewed news to a short video app.

At a management retreat in Japan, Yiming Zhang decided that the time was right. It wasn't a difficult decision. In 2016, short video was everywhere – not just in China, but worldwide. Vine was in its heyday, and there was a small army of short-form apps popular in China. King among them was an app called Kwai, run by a company called Kuaishou.

Zhang handpicked Kelly Zhang (no relation) to launch the new app. She knew that it would have to be different from the rest, and ByteDance spent months thinking carefully about how it could stand out against the competition. Key to its thinking was a motto from Sun Tzu's *Art of War*: 'If you know the enemy and know yourself, you need not fear the result of a hundred battles.' The team took it literally, downloading 100 different short-form video apps from around the world onto their phones and trying each one out. That 100 included Alex Zhu's Musical.ly, which was out in the United States but wouldn't arrive in China until May 2017.

None of what the developers saw impressed them. They reckoned they could do better.

The small team scoping out the short-form video market started to list what irked them about the apps on the market, some of which had millions of users. They managed to narrow it down to four key areas of friction they felt they could improve.

One of the things that they disliked was the way most of the apps handled the video. It was relegated to a small corner of the screen, or obscured by lots of on-screen clutter. Some were landscape, and unless you tilted your phone, became infinitesimally small on a smartphone screen. Others were square, which was better, but still not the best use of precious screen real estate. They also noticed some of the apps they used seemed to scrimp on server costs, producing fuzzy video in their app. (High definition video uses up a lot of data, and ultimately, that data has to be stored somewhere.) The developers tried out different configurations, and came to the conclusion that if they were going to do a video app, it would have to be full screen and high definition – which just so happened to be the same thought Zhu and Musical.ly had nearly two years earlier.

Kelly Zhang also wanted her app to be different from the rest of the online video world by focusing on music – to such an extent that the app ended up adopting the cumbersome slogan 'a music short video community for young people' when it launched. Music was key, ByteDance believed, because of the way that people interacted with their smartphones. By the mid-2010s, what we first thought of as an unusual sight of people walking down the street with two white earpieces stuffed into their ears was becoming commonplace. Surveys of users of ByteDance's other apps suggested that music was a constant in their lives, and that it was something they would want in a short video app, too.

Another constant in the lives of image-obsessed Chinese youngsters was the ability to pluck and preen and smooth out blemishes through filters. Filters were particularly popular in China, where the idea of bending your face and body to unnaturally slender proportions was acceptable. ByteDance's researchers determined that there was likely to be little interest in a short video app among Chinese youngsters if they were presented in the cold, harsh light of reality, rather than the idealised selves they could conjure up on other apps. The team also knew that the algorithmic superpower of Toutiao could distinguish its new app from competitors.

Every other app seemed to make users jump through a different set of hoops, and didn't let them dive headlong into creating their own videos. ByteDance wanted to make it as easy as possible to start filming videos, reasoning that any additional effort required would put people off. It left nothing to chance, even thinking about the best way to ensure videos went viral, and developing the concept of hashtag challenges, which have become popular since.

ByteDance still needed a name for its new app, and so it put out the call companywide for suggestions. The team considered hundreds. The initial choice was A.me. But while the name worked in English, where people conflated it with 'awesome,' it didn't in Chinese. After a few months the winner was Douyin – which combines the verb 'to shake' (dou) and the word 'sound' (yin) to create a word that means 'vibrato.'

The logo was created by a 24-year-old designer who had a love of rock music, and who was inspired by the ringing sensation in his ears after a concert and the strobing sensation in his eyes as a result of the stupendous light show that closed out the gig. He sketched a logo inspired by a musical note, then ran it through an animated GIF generator that added an electromagnetic wave. Forty separate frames resulted from the GIF, and the designer picked out the cleanest-looking one, which presented the logo in hazy electric blue (called 'Splash' in TikTok's internal graphical style book) and pinky-red (nicknamed 'Razzmatazz') shadow.

Douyin was born.

In September 2016, it was ready to launch after months of development. At first, Douyin bumped along, not making significant waves. But ByteDance employees kept tinkering. It founded an AI Lab within the company to help develop the augmented reality stickers and filters that would bring users back to the app again and again. It engaged with one particularly outspoken user called Mr Xue, a student at a Canadian university who used a VPN to access the China-only app, who was unhappy with a slight lag between speech and video in Douyin. By mid-2017 things were starting to pick up. Some of the hashtag challenges that Douyin developed in collaboration with its early adopters started cutting through to the mainstream, including one called the shower dance, developed by two of the platform's keenest users. 'It's very important to create this kind of opportunity to approach users,' said Kelly Zhang. In the early days, ByteDance would even invite Douyin's most ardent users into the offices to chat and create videos together. Its creator-centric approach would soon power TikTok's arrival in the West.

11
LAUNCH
OF TIKTOK

ByteDance soon wanted to launch a Western version of Douyin, which could be even freer. In May 2017, ByteDance launched an early version of TikTok on the Google Play Store, which most Android phone owners worldwide used to download apps, and targeted growth in Asia first. TikTok opened a sixth-floor shared office space in Shibuya, Tokyo. Slowly, TikTok found a foothold by acclimatising to the local culture. Many videos were ported over from Douyin to TikTok and augmented with Japanese-shot videos. Simultaneously, TikTok expanded into Thailand, Taiwan, Indonesia and Vietnam.

As well as borrowing content from Douyin, TikTok heavily relied on its code. As a team of academics who analysed the differences between the global and Chinese versions of the app put it, 'TikTok and Douyin are twin sibling platforms separated at birth; developed under one roof but deployed in vastly different contexts.' You could see the similarities by opening up your phone's app store. Type the word 'TikTok' into the search bar and you saw – and still can see – the logo that has become an icon for many of the app's users. A stylised quaver that looked like it's been run through a series of filters that jolts it right to left and leaves a slight echo of blue and red interference on either side, TikTok's logo has become synonymous with fun and fame in the last two years.

Take a flight to China, type in the word 'Douyin' into the same app store search bar, and you would come across an app with the same electro-shocked logo on a black, rounded square background. Nothing was different.

And that was by design. They were both the same on the surface, with the same owner. Thrown headlong into an endless stream of videos, you would see a string of icons down the right hand of the screen underneath the user's profile photo. These allowed you to like, comment on and share the video. The whole thing was designed to be a little disorientating, aimed at capturing your attention with a bravura sweep of the ecosystem, showing its creativity, anarchy and vibrancy.

But there was a hidden simplicity behind the appearance of a lot happening, too. TikTok and Douyin were engineered to make it as easy as possible for users to like, engage with, and share content – often outside the app, which was a vital part of its livelihood. Part of TikTok's popularity came from canny early adopters cherry-picking the best bits and reposting them using the built-in share function on the app onto other platforms like Facebook and Twitter, where they gained an audience often larger than the views seen on TikTok itself. See enough of the watermarked TikTok videos on Twitter, ByteDance thought, and a holdout may give up and end up trying TikTok out themselves. 'These platforms are able to reach and draw in new audiences by enabling easy shareability of their content on other platforms,' says Zoe Glatt, a researcher at the London School of Economics, who coaxed me into attending the TikTok session at VidCon. 'They control the marketing narrative by watermarking their content when it is downloaded.'

It's not just in engagement and sharing that TikTok and Douyin sought to reduce friction as much as possible. One of the biggest innovations was the way both apps made easy what was thought to be a highly complicated process of creating videos. Becoming a major YouTuber was a challenge, not least because of the amount of effort involved in creating a video. For TikTok and Douyin, it was not. We'll show how creators have exploited this ease in some personal stories later.

But it's important to note that, like siblings, in their first year TikTok and Douyin diverged in key ways. TikTok and Douyin gave a different prominence to livestreaming. The livestreaming community was well-established in China; TikTok reflected the Western world where livestreaming was still seen as an additional extra, rather than a core component of a digital creator's life. From the moment Douyin was launched it bombarded users with live content, while on TikTok live video only came into its own with some live concerts it staged to keep people entertained at home during the coronavirus lockdown.

What happened in those livestreams was also different: in China, audiences happily donated money to their favourite creators to thank them. In the West, the donation capabilities existed on TikTok, but were much less prominent and not well-used. (One relatively large TikToker who had been on the app for months only realised she had been receiving money from her audience when she delved into the deepest corners of the app's interface. And even then, she hadn't even earned enough from her fans to afford a fast food meal.)

On the Discover tab on the app – a list of trending hashtags and content on the platform – was a more revealing difference. In TikTok there was a standard, single page of trending content to choose from. On Douyin that sat alongside another subsection called *zheng nengliang*: 'positive energy.'

'Positive energy' also showed trending videos, but these ones were different. They were selected from a corner of Douyin that presents videos promoting the ruling Chinese communist party and their societal ideals. ByteDance developed the positive energy section after having to shut down another of its apps, Neihan Duanzi, a meme repository, because it supposedly posted vulgar content. ByteDance apologised to the ruling party and to the people for such a terrible misjudgement, and simultaneously inserted the positive energy tab into Douyin. Academics and analysts called it a 'survival tactic,' placating the politicians who could shut down the business on a whim. Yet it showed how ultimately, although the same core mechanisms run both apps, there were fundamental differences between them because of their very different operating environments.

Another was the filters users could put on their videos to make them more appealing. Open the default camera filter on TikTok and your skin tone appeared to be natural. Open it on Douyin and your face appeared to be lighter – a consequence of a Chinese cultural norm called *meibai*, or beautify whitening, that has plagued apps for years. That extended into the deep library of filters available to tweak any video. While TikTok largely remained focussed around basic filters and the opportunity to overlay memes and stickers, Douyin's raft of filters were fixated on looks – a good number of them widened eyes, lightened skin, and heightened cheekbones. That reflected the predominant thinking in society:

many Chinese people fixate on Westernising their features, with some even taking drastic steps, spending thousands of pounds on plastic surgery to have paler skin, wider eyes and higher cheekbones. But it demonstrated the way that ByteDance was willing to adapt to the culture and rules of the relevant society.

12
PAYING
FOR POPULARITY

Yiming Zhang wanted to expand rapidly into markets around the world and realised that the secret to success in any country depended on achieving critical mass quickly. One way to achieve that was by advertising. ByteDance bankrolled a nearly unprecedented public advertising campaign, spending millions of dollars a day on digital and television advertising. And in a developing country it found it could, quite cheaply, win over the poorer working classes in the smaller cities before pushing into the wealthier urban centres.

In India, for instance – which we'll use as a case study of TikTok's march to global dominance – ByteDance knew that the less-well-educated members of Indian society often lived in 'tier 4 and 5 cities.' One former ByteDance employee in India, explaining the country's city tier system, said: 'They don't know much about English content, or posh or good content. They just want to see some village comedy, people dancing on some random song – that stuff.'

Because the inhabitants of these cities were poor, uneducated and didn't have much disposable income, they were not usually attractive to advertisers. That meant TikTok could target them very cheaply. The so-called CPM (clicks per mille) for people in tier 4 and 5 cities was incredibly low. Digital adverts on Facebook and YouTube and Google search results showed potential customers a new app called TikTok they might want to download. Many did. ByteDance flooded the app with 'shadow accounts' – fake accounts created by the app makers that upload the kind of content enjoyed by users.

That gave the app momentum. It pushed a huge number of people onto TikTok, catapulting it up the app store charts and bringing it to the attention of journalists. The content that the users were creating might not be perfect – it was more likely than not the kind of 'cringe content' that put off more highbrow users – but it populated the app nonetheless. 'When you target tier 4 and 5 cities, they give you the number of downloads, the user numbers, and some cringe content,' the former ByteDance employee said.

Once TikTok reached a critical mass of users in those smaller, lower-class cities, towns and villages, it started expanding its horizons. ByteDance ploughed money into targeting microinfluencers on other apps who lived in tier 3 cities – the middle-class members of Indian society who are hobbyist creators on social media platforms and straddle the line between everyday users and more committed, professional creators. These tier 3 microinfluencers might have 5,000 or 10,000 followers on Instagram, and could be lured over to the new app with a small amount of money and the promise of being in on a runaway success from the start.

That new influx of users changed the makeup of the app. So-called cringe content – the low-quality, grainy footage bobbing around as one friend shakily films another as they dance along to an old Bollywood favourite – was slowly replaced by higher quality content acceptable to wealthier users. Once that type of content made up around a third of all the videos on the app, ByteDance targeted tier 2 cities, which had large numbers of inhabitants but weren't the country's biggest. The company contacted major influencers on Instagram – those with a million followers or more, who make videos with good lighting, makeup and sound, offering them payments running into the thousands of dollars to join TikTok. At the same time, it also invested more into traditional marketing, designing campaigns that highlighted the app's good points for users of Instagram and YouTube. Once enough professional influencers had been lured over to the app, ByteDance then ramped up its marketing budget and spent more on attracting bona fide traditional celebrities.

Such celebrities unlocked an extra audience. They brought brand name recognition within a section of the population who perhaps dipped in and out of platforms, rather than logging on every single minute of the day.

When TikTok achieves critical mass, as it did in India, people of all ages want to join in. In late 2018 and early 2019, for instance, Geetha Sridhar, a 54-year-old mother from Mumbai, wondered why her daughter Sarada and her older sister were glued to their smartphones, performing skits and choreographed dances. She asked what it was, and when she found out, asked if she could join in with her daughters.

The mother ended up taking part in a few dances her daughters choreographed and filmed – but didn't post publicly, instead keeping the videos private on the app. They didn't want to embarrass their mum, and worried that once out there, she may want them brought back offline, which is easier said than done. They needn't have worried. Geetha asked her daughters to install

TikTok on her phone, so she didn't have to pester them when she wanted to record a video.

Geetha built up a career as a chef and a food blogger, and began taking her phone with her when she reviewed restaurants, recording and posting interviews with the chefs. When she got home, she'd appear with her daughters in their dance videos.

People loved Geetha, and the idea that a middle-aged Indian woman who had a seemingly endless supply of colourful saris, would end up being such an avid TikToker. 'At her age, she dances with so much expression and passion that people enjoyed it,' explained Sarada. First a few thousand clicked the follow button on her profile. Then it was 100,000. Then half a million. By June 2020, Geetha was about to get her millionth fan. She was posting dozens of videos every day. 'People were enjoying the no-age barrier,' said Sarada.

Another unexpected star of Indian TikTok was Hydroman, whose videos take place inside a bright light blue tank. Wearing dark blue goggles, or occasionally large, thin-rimmed glasses, the only clue that Jaydeep Gohil is submerged underwater comes when you spot the thin bit of plastic that pinches his nostrils closed, and when you start to see his thick black quiff waft from side to side, pushed by the current of the water. Hydroman, who started on YouTube then migrated to TikTok, then starts dancing and lip syncing along to some of Bollywood's most popular songs, his movements slowed to an elegant drift by the drag of the water inside his custom-built tank.

Gohil's videos tick all the TikTok boxes: your trigger-happy scrolling finger hovers for a moment as your eyes try to comprehend what you're seeing. Then he starts moving – the twist in the tale – before seamlessly conducting his dance and singing along in sync to the song. It's a Disney film come to life in front of your eyes. It's unbelievable. It's unexpected. It's a dopamine hit. You must tell your friends.

And when Indians did tell their friends on other social channels such as Facebook, TikTok had a way to make them remember where the video they enjoyed first appeared. TikTok was always happy for its videos to be downloaded and posted on other social media platforms – say in a tweet. Because in the corner of each downloaded video was a watermark showing the TikTok logo and the profile name of the original poster. The idea – used by Flipagram – was that some of the millions who watched a TikTok on Twitter or Facebook would notice the name of the app, download it from the app store, and try it out themselves.

13
TAKEOVER OF
MUSICAL.LY

Watermarking didn't exist in Musical.ly until it was redesigned in April 2015. When it was introduced, it was a game changer. Within two months, Musical.ly had gone from being around the 1,250th most popular app on the US Apple app store, to the most popular. Numbers grew until the app had roughly a million monthly active users – enough to bring in futher funding of $16.6 million by August 2015. By then, in contrast to ByteDance, Musical.ly was reputedly not spending a penny to distribute itself. It had become what Zhu wanted it to be: 'a blank canvas for this young generation, and to provide a lot of tools to allow them creative expression.' New features were added all the time. A location filter called My City allowed users to find locally created videos. And in 2016, an algorithm better ranked and exposed videos – adding in what Zhu himself called 'a market economy' to an environment that was previously run as 'a planning economy.'

Musical.ly was booming and, despite being Chinese-owned, was most popular in Europe and North America, the markets in which TikTok was weakest. By contrast, TikTok was strongest in Asia. Nearly nine in 10 users were in Japan, Thailand, Taiwan, Indonesia and Vietnam.

Zhang's TikTok decided to strike and took over Musical.ly in November 2017, paying $800 million. The deal massively expanded TikTok's reach. 'We are excited to enter into a new chapter,' said Alex Zhu, who had spent years building up Musical.ly, and whose app had just accumulated 100 million monthly active users. 'TikTok, the sound of a ticking clock, represents the short nature of the video platform. Combining Musical.ly and TikTok is a natural fit given the shared mission of both experiences – to create a community where everyone can be a creator.'

The deal was a good fit, though there was still an obstacle to come: merging the apps and switching Musical.ly's users over to TikTok. It took almost nine months for the change to be enacted, but when it did, it was lightning quick. On 1 August 2018, TikTok published a statement on their website saying the two apps were merging, and Musical.ly would be subsumed into TikTok. On 2 August 2018, Musical.ly's users awoke and switched on their phone screens to see its iconic logo, a red circle with a curved sound wave streaking across its horizon, had disappeared. In its place stood TikTok's vibrating musical note on a black background.

Some were happy. Some were sad. Some were resigned to the change, while others were defiant. One, Brian Bertoline, tweeted: 'Musical.ly is now 'TikTok,' but I will always be a Muser. Not a clock.' That anger subsided. Bertoline ended up taking the forced migration to TikTok in his stride. The Philadelphia teenager still posts on TikTok today, each video getting a few hundred views.

Now the stage was set for Zhang's ByteDance to attempt global video domination. It would be achieved with two apps, each catering for its specific operating environment: Douyin in communist China and TikTok in the capitalist West.

CREATOR FOCUS
ANNA

Name: Anna Bogomolova
Username: @anna
Following: 394
Followers: 2.4M
Likes: 103.8M
Speciality: Harnessing the latest trends and creating amazing makeup transformations

A song by a YouTube star propelled Anna Bogomolova to fame on TikTok.

The year was 2018, and Thomas 'Tomska' Ridgewell, a veteran You-Tuber with six million subscribers, had released a bizarre song with an accompanying animated video that told the story of an anthropomor-phised muffin begging to be eaten. (The song, in case it wasn't imme-diately clear, isn't just a little ditty about muffins. Ridgewell is one of the most open and eloquent advocates for mental health and the pressure on digital creators, which the song deals with.) The high-pitched voice of the muffin asks the people he encounters to eat him, saying: 'Please I wanna die, die, die,' to a jovial tune portrayed in a cutesy cartoon that includes a choreographed dance with backing singers – who are also muffins.

It was an odd piece of internet ephemera that captures the essence of what makes the digital world so enthralling. It balanced light and shade, was smart and funny and popular. In a little over two years, it's been seen 181 million times on YouTube.

The song was a smash hit online, and Bogomolova was one of the millions who saw it. She had first signed up to Musical.ly after encountering an ad for the app on Facebook in March 2016 as a 17-year-old. She wasn't that big on Musical.ly, and while she had navigated the transition to TikTok better than many of the arty lip syncers she associated with on the app, dozens of whom departed when Musical.ly became TikTok, she still wasn't huge on TikTok.

Until *Muffin Time* hit. Bogomolova liked the song and thought it could make for an interesting lip sync. She took a 15-second snippet of *Muffin Time* and recorded a bizarre video to accompany it. While singing about being a muffin and wanting to be eaten, the short, blonde-haired girl with her hair in pigtails who borrows heavily from Japan's *kawaii* (cute) culture pranced about like a madwoman in a pink tutu. The fisheye lens she used for the video compounded the sense of strangeness, and accentuated the small dots she painted on her cheekbones – doll-like make-up that she often sports.

In the weird world of the internet economy, the video took on a life of its own, being reposted on YouTube and Instagram even after it was taken down by TikTok's community moderators. (Bogomolova believes that the video might have fallen victim to an overly censorious moderator who didn't like the moment that she put the lens down her throat, allowing the audience full view of her tonsils.) PewDiePie, the world's biggest individual YouTuber, posted a reaction video where he expressed his befuddlement at Bogomolova's TikTok. It drew people to her profile.

In the end, 1.5 million people watched her video on TikTok, and millions more on other apps. Because the original video was initially taken down for being inappropriate, the video Bogomolova had posted just before that, where she transformed in a split second from lip syncing to a popular song in slobby clothes to the same tutu-and-top outfit, became a big beneficiary of the additional audience, getting 2.5 million views.

From averaging just a few thousand views after upload, Bogomolova suddenly could reliably count on hundreds of thousands, if not millions, of people engaging with her content. She had made it on TikTok, and TikTok wanted to meet her.

A few months later, while at VidCon London 2019, the company's community managers came up to her breathlessly and praised her content – specifically the *Muffin Time* video. 'I told them the video got taken down,' she says. 'They didn't know how it happened. But they put it back up.'

Bogomolova knew that pleasing the algorithm was important, and so spent her first few weeks post-merger monitoring what kind of videos the newly christened TikTok seemed to like. She found that it was less lip syncing, and more trend-based, rapidly reacting videos.

Many of her peers from Musical.ly also made the transition, but they didn't adapt. Like the dinosaurs, they found themselves suddenly outmoded and out of favour with the all-powerful algorithm. They continued promoting their lip syncing videos, and found that the videos weren't getting much engagement. Out of a friendship group of maybe 30 or so from her Musical.ly days, only four or five now still post on TikTok.

Aged 23, Bogomolova sometimes finds it difficult to manage the balance between chasing views and doing what she wants on the plat-form. While it's work, and has brought her some income through brand deals and sponsorships, she also wants it to be fun. 'I try to somehow find a compromise between what I want to do and what they're looking for,' she says. She knows that's a more pragmatic approach than some. 'It depends on where your priorities are: whether you want to express yourself as a creator and a creative or if you want a big following.' And besides, she says, 'if you don't have an audience, who are you making videos for?'

Bogomolova is constantly scanning the horizon looking for trends she can exploit. She does very little planning. Instead, she dives head-long into the For You page like the rest of us, sees what's happening, and decides on her strategy for that day. 'Just looking through, I figure out what I'm going to do and what I'm going to film,' she says. If some-thing doesn't work the first time round, she can simply try again: she's wasted at most, 60 seconds of her time. So far it's paid off.

CREATOR FOCUS
FREYA FOX

Name: Freya Fox
Username: @freyafoxgg
Following: 1,124
Followers: 50,400
Likes: 146,700
Speciality: Gaming and electronic dance music

'I think I probably have the most unique story that you'll ever hear,' says Freya Fox, 'because I was aware of TikTok before it was even TikTok, and before it was Musical.ly.' The professional gaming streamer lived in Asia from 2016 to 2018, right at the time that Douyin, the Chinese equivalent of TikTok, was burying its claws into the brains of the population there.

Fox lived in Taiwan at the time, and saw the popularity of the app among the Chinese-speaking app. 'Everybody was saying: "Look at this new social media app, Douyin",' she recalls. At the time, the app was still relatively rudimentary: the majority of the userbase, like TikTok in its early days in the West, were lip syncers and dancers. It wasn't Fox's cup of tea to join in with creating videos, but like millions of others she became glued to her phone as a viewer.

The gamer moved back to the United States in 2018, and soon after used the western version of TikTok for the first time. The reason? 'It was the in thing to do at the time, and I've always been an early adopter of tech in general,' she says. 'So I wanted to get in on it, and be among the first to use it.'

There was one problem: contractually she wasn't allowed to devote too much time to developing a TikTok following – the result of signing a deal as a partner with Facebook Gaming, who asked her to prioritise her content for its platform, rather than competitors. When the deal lapsed in 2019, she gravitated towards TikTok more seriously, seeing it starting to rise in the public's consciousness and deciding she could still make her imprint on it.

By 2020 and the start of the coronavirus pandemic, TikTok had firmly cemented itself as the way to waste time spent at home as countries locked down their borders, their shops, and all their entertainment.

Fox had become involved in the cryptocurrency investing world, and saw people start to talk about the rise of crypto coins such as Dogecoin after Elon Musk tweeted about them earlier that year. In the same way that people were exchanging trading tips about how to beat the old financial system on the WallStreetBets subreddit, at the same time she saw plenty of TikTok users swapping advice about investing.

'2020 and 2021 were really weird and unique years because I felt like the majority of content on TikTok – at least that I was seeing – was investing advice,' Fox says. 'It was financial stuff.' She believes that a large driver of the change was the shifting demographics of TikTok's userbase: while the young teenagers who had first propelled the app into the public consciousness by giving it the imprimatur of the next big thing were still there, their parents and older siblings had also joined. 'You started seeing a lot more entrepreneurs and business owners and musicians taking it seriously,' she says. 'They were suddenly realising this was the platform you can grow on.'

Among them is Fox herself. She's done well from TikTok, gaining a devoted following of 50,000 who follow her for her gaming and DJ performances on the app. She posts regular TikToks, but has made good use of the livestreaming tools TikTok offers, called TikTok Live. She'll regularly start streaming footage of her playing video games from her brightly-lit gaming room in Las Vegas late at night, encouraging her audience to interact with her through the text chat that runs alongside it. It's given her an audience, and offline fame, too: her TikTok Live popularity has led to bookings at major music festivals alongside Snoop Dogg and Megan Thee Stallion, in large part thanks to working with a manager within TikTok whose job it is to support live streamers on the app.

One late night, she set a stretch target for her audience: if they got her to a certain number of followers or likes, she'd cut her hair. She's seen the bubbling up of the app, and its cooling off too. 'It really shifted in 2021, and now in 2022, you've seen a decline in organic reach,' she says. 'It's not as easy to grow anymore.'

Fox compares what her For You Page looked like in 2020 and 2021 to now. 'Back then, any mom and pop, any Joe Schmoe, anybody could be on your For You Page and pop off,' she says. 'Now it's more obvious that the people that are on your For You Page are professionals and have this very high-quality content.'

That's not a good nor a bad thing, she points out – it's just different. 'It's pretty basic supply and demand,' she says. But she sees a growing wave of professionalisation on the platform that reminds her of another company that became a major player in the online video space: YouTube. 'You've seen a big push in advertising and brand collabs, and things like that,' she says. 'It's gone the way of YouTube where it's very obvious that content choices are being driven with advertising in mind first.'

PART III

THE GROWTH OF TIKTOK

14
THE SECRETS
OF SUCCESS

Douyin and TikTok spread around the world rapidly, thanks to their in-depth analysis of competitors and intense focus on detail. But in terms of their features, two interconnected things in particular distinguished them from their competitors. The first was the length of the videos, and the second was the algorithm used to serve up those videos.

First, video length. Attention spans are plastic, malleable things, shaped by the world around us. Take away all the distractions – the bawl of a young baby needing to be fed, the mental checklist of tasks to do and the looming deadline for a big work project, and it's possible to immerse yourself in a book like this that tells a long, detailed narrative. But pile each of those distractions up, one on top of another, and you start to see your ability to concentrate rapidly run away. It's something scientists have long studied, and worried about: does the torrent of information we're presented with daily stunt our ability to think deeply and engage with something for longer than a few seconds?

Apparently so: Canadian researchers studied the attention spans of 2,000 people at the turn of the millennium, and did the same experiment 15 years later. In the intervening years – which saw the rapid rollout of home computers, the advent of YouTube and the iPhone, and the rise in availability and fall in cost of affordable home broadband internet – our ability to concentrate on one thing before our brain switched off dropped by a third, from 12 seconds to eight. It's not just in terms of immediate concerns that we're able to concentrate only for a short period. A long-term analysis by separate researchers shows that an abundance of information is correlated with exhausting our attention. 'Our urge for newness causes us to collectively switch topics more rapidly,' said a researcher at the Max Planck Institute for Human Development.

The same social platforms that have been in part responsible for shortening our attention spans are also helping feed the newly gnat-like focus we can offer. And TikTok is fine-tuned to capture our attention for just as long as it can, before serving us up the next nugget of video it knows will keep us scrolling. According to the app's head of content partnerships, most videos are a 15- to 30-second burst of truncated joy, forcing those creating the content to be as creative as they can be in a short period of time. Internal guidance to new creators advises them to post videos lasting between 11 and 17 seconds long, and longer than 10 seconds at a minimum. In the new world of TikTok, Andy Warhol's infamous 15 minutes of fame have, quite literally, become 15 seconds.

Think about the amount of content it's possible to consume in an hour on TikTok. If each video lasts 60 seconds maximum, that's 60 videos, back-to-back, encountering 60 new faces and opening a door into their world – and an opportunity to follow them further and propel them to superstardom. Contrast that to YouTube, where the average length of videos is getting longer and longer as more and more of us stop snatching views on the move and instead settle down on the sofa to watch feature-length documentaries, and it's much harder to build a following. TikTok's video length also hits the sweet spot: you're unlikely to get bored quickly, instead constantly grazing on new, outlandish content – that has been designed by its creators to grab your attention immediately and offer you a novel twist to give you a dopamine hit that'll carry you through to the next video.

It's for that reason that TikTok has proven so popular. You're never going to get bored when meticulously chosen videos are presented at your fingertips in an endless scroll, that you can flick by at will.

The second factor that has propelled TikTok is its algorithm. It powers not just TikTok, but all of ByteDance's products, and is the money maker for the entire company. Indeed, ByteDance has been commercially exploiting the mechanism that delivers its content and other technology in its apps, such as image recognition and computer vision. In China, ByteDance has sold white labelled versions of its algorithm and other tools under the brand name Volcengine for more than a year, while, in April 2021, insiders told me, it began hiring staff in Singapore to sell the same systems to Western companies under the brand name BytePlus.

Like YouTube's algorithm, which dictates who makes it and who doesn't, TikTok's algorithm is complicated and largely mysterious, to outsiders and even to many insiders. When I asked Yazmin How, TikTok's editorial lead in the UK, how it worked, she was nonplussed. 'It's a question I don't think even the algo team have the answer to,' she said. 'It's just so sophisticated.'

Yet there are pointers on how to make an algorithm-friendly video. 'It needs to be filmed with good light,' How said. 'It needs some decent quality. It doesn't need to be super-polished. Ninety-nine percent of the content we see going viral is authentic to the platform, and making things that are real.' TikTok is an app firmly rooted in the attention economy – and if you don't grab a user's interest quickly, you aren't going anywhere fast. How said: 'If the first three seconds suck you in as a user, you're more likely to finish the video and then that will be served out to more and more people.'

Just as with YouTube's often-anxious creators who are always striving to try and reverse engineer how its algorithm works, so TikTok's nascent creator base spends some of its time trying to figure out how to game the system to obtain the biggest possible chance of fame. Almost all videos posted on the app by people wanting to find an audience have the word #fyp appended to the caption, the legacy of a misguided belief that anything that isn't tagged with that won't end up on the main place to discover videos in the app.

But beyond that, few people have much insight into what exactly TikTok's algorithm looks for – or more accurately put, how it's coded to operate. (One of the biggest issues with algorithms on social media platforms is that they're imbued with a personality by people desperate to figure out how to strike it lucky. In reality, they are just computer code running on cold logic.)

As with many things about TikTok, the platform's relative youth means that the range of algorithm whisperers who think they know how the system operates is smaller than the growth-hacking community that thrives on YouTube, hosting events at industry conferences that promise to boost a user's standing on the site. But those algorithm experts still exist, testing different inputs to see if they can figure out what exactly the app prioritises and why.

Among them is VEED, a video editing app, which claims that TikTok looks at all videos posted on its platform through two computerised lenses. First it looks at the video using natural language processing – the things you say, and the things you type in the caption of the video – as well as through computer vision technology, trying to identify what you're doing, where you are, and how the video evolves, and translating it into computer-readable checklists. That understanding comes from a ByteDance spokesperson, who gave a hint about the app's inner workings by saying 'we build intelligent machines that are capable of understanding and analysing text, images and videos using natural language processing and computer vision technology.' Doing so enables the company to serve content that users find most interesting.

But TikTok won't show a video to all its users immediately. The app relies on its users seeing TikTok as a place of endless entertainment. Any videos that aren't up to the same high standard that's expected, broadcast to a broad audience, are likely to lower their view of the app's quality. So instead, once it has analysed the content of the video using its computer-aided AI through the two lenses, it will send it out to a small number of users to gauge their reaction.

It's at this point, when the video is tested out on a fragment of TikTok's vast userbase, that the video reaches its pivotal moment. The reaction of those few users who are served the video in their feeds will dictate the future of the video: whether it'll be a soaring success, put into millions of For You feeds, or a flop, destined to remain unloved and unwatched. And that trial run is important, because the For You page is a vitally important part of the app.

'Part of the magic of TikTok is that there's no one For You feed,' the company explains. 'While different people may come upon some of the same standout videos, each person's feed is unique and tailored to that specific individual.'

Those reactions are measured in a number of ways, and it appears that TikTok uses a hierarchy to differentiate between interesting and boring videos. Videos that are watched all the way through and/or rewatched multiple times are given the most weight in being recommended.

The next most important metric to decide whether a video should be pushed out from a small test number of users to the broader TikTok community is whether it's been shared using the app's interface. Comments are the next most important weighting when it comes to deciding which videos are attractive, while someone double-tapping on a video to indicate they like it is the least valuable indication a video is worth pushing out to more people.

All of these components, which are meant to estimate the audience's enjoyment of a particular video, are calculated together to give a score. If that score meets a certain unknown threshold, the video will be pushed out into the world to be seen by a wider range of TikTok users. The process of scoring a video based on its rewatchability, comments, likes, shares and so on is repeated with that range of users and the video becomes more and more viral, until people lose interest, and the video drops off the For You page.

What's interesting is that unlike many other social media platforms, chiefly YouTube, which keep serving up their biggest creators to users on a regular basis, TikTok tries to share the love (or perhaps to generate an army of strong performers, rather than a few, powerful mega-stars). 'While a video is likely to receive more views if posted by an account that has more followers, by virtue of that account having built up a larger follower base, neither follower count nor whether the account has had previous high-performing videos are direct factors in the recommendation system,' the company claims. In fact, it's keen to try and avoid filter bubbles, and endless loops of being served the same types of videos by the same sorts of creators. The app's feed has failed if it shows a user two videos in a row with the same backing track, or produced by the same creator.

Each one of those data points is also used to build up a picture of every user. When you open TikTok for the first time, the app will fire some of the most popular content at your eyeballs through the home screen, and will see on which videos you dwell, which ones you skip past, and which ones you watch over and over again. Every one of those decisions – down to the very split second you spend on a video – builds up a picture of who you are and what you like. That picture is constantly updated and fine-tuned depending on the time of day, where you're based when you open the app, and a multitude of other options, meaning that every time you reopen the app, the slate of new videos presented to you is designed to better match your interests.

I've seen that myself. When I've written about the ranks of people performing TikToks while at work in Tesco and other supermarkets, my TikTok algorithm has adapted. Because I've gone and sought out those videos, and rewatched them time and time again, TikTok thinks I like supermarket videos. And so I get videos of people riding their trolleys down supermarket aisles, freewheeling between the cheese and the butter. When I added another variable to my watching while researching a story on people performing hashtag challenges while standing in queues for shops during the coronavirus outbreak, TikTok thought it could triangulate what it believed was one of my interests – supermarkets – with another, queues. Soon it was giving me videos of people queueing not outside shops, but inside supermarkets. Those kinds of queueing videos are of shops based in the UK, because the app tends to take into account where the user is based when deciding what videos to show them, alongside other elements like the type of device they use.

It's all in aid of one of TikTok's main goals: reducing friction. The more effort you have to make to find the videos you like, the less likely you are to return to it time and time again. By making sure it knows you, and serves you high quality videos on a constantly loop, TikTok is trying to prevent you ever abandoning it.

TikTok knows the power of its algorithm – and the addictive nature of its endless scroll. In February 2020, users across the world started seeing strange videos appearing on their For You page. One of them, a 17-year-old called Leena, encountered one of the videos around 11pm one evening, two hours after she had opened up the app and hurled herself into the video feed. She was greeted by a broad grinning, handsome young man with expressive eyebrows and wrinkles around his eyes from laughing. 'I understand it's easy to keep watching videos,' the man beseeched her through the camera lens. 'And trust me, I've been there before. But those videos will still be there tomorrow. Go get some extra sleep, turn your phone off, do yourself that favour, and have a great night.'

The man was TikToker Gabe Erwin, who at the time had two million followers on the app, and he was posting from an account that wasn't his normal one. @TikTokTips was set up by the company to try and counteract claims that it was trying to hook its often-young userbase. Some of the platform's biggest names recorded specialised videos encouraging people to put down their phones. One, by Cosette Rinab, a bubbly blonde girl whose video thumbnails always highlight gleeful, over-the-top expressions that even the most hammy silent movie starlet would shirk at, got straight to the point: 'When's the last time you've been outside?', she suggested to those watching.

Asking people to switch off TikTok may seem like a counterintuitive decision, but it generates some positive PR, and heads off criticism that it is capitalising on the attention economy. One social media academic who studies the way apps use 'dark patterns,' or design tricks that are aimed at keeping you hooked, said it was an example of TikTok having its cake and eating it. 'They first build knowingly addictive patterns into the core of their app, then add patterns that, while quite paternalistic, also make it seem as if they are being good internet citizens,' says Colin Gray, a lecturer at Purdue University in the US. Just how addictive those patterns are can be seen by monitoring how a handful of people use the app.

15
HOW WE
USE TIKTOK

Taha Shakil doesn't remember 8 June 2020 as anything out of the ordinary. It was just a regular Monday for the marketing specialist from Toronto, Canada. Though the data captured by TikTok showing how he interacted with the app over that 24 hours – which Shakil shared with me for this book and which any TikTok user can download through the app – tells a different story. 'I was pretty shocked, but not surprised at the data collected by TikTok,' Shakil told me after handing over the data. 'I work in advertising, so all the targeting options large companies offer to us, have to come from somewhere. Privacy is now a thing of the past.'

Shakil must have woken up during the night: at 2.27am, he unlocked his iPhone 11 and opened up TikTok. The first video he was served up by TikTok's algorithm was from Zahraa Berro, a Muslim beauty blogger with 171,000 followers, living in Laguna Beach, California, who specialises in so-called 'modest fashion.' The video, about how to thread stray hairs from your upper lip, which Berro had been doing for eight years, rather than going to her local mall's beauty counter, seemed to interest Shakil a little bit. He lingered for 12 seconds on the 15-second video before flicking on to the next one.

There, he encountered Sarvenaz Myslicki, vice president of engineering at LinkedIn, giving career advice about how to field the tricky question many job applicants face in an interview: Why do you want to leave your current job? The video's a slick one, with heavy use of TikTok's filters: at one point, Myslicki appears in a graphical representation of hell to represent the bad answer, and among clouds and angels, an augmented reality halo over her head, when providing the more positive answer. Shakil watched the video for its entire duration, before scrolling on again.

Next he saw Krystle Byrne, a lifeguard at a local pool in Charlotte County, Florida, as she removed her flipflops and waded into the water of the pool she oversees. 'I'm fed up with life so today is the day I decided I'm meant to be a drowning victim not the hero,' she says in the caption. Shakil was one of 14.6 million people to have watched it. After that, he was served an ad by TikTok's algorithm promoting a game called Eternal Sword M – although the big, on-stage screen playing in-game footage behind the woman presenting information about the game calls it 'Eteranl.' Shakil isn't enamoured by the video, or the game: he moved on within three seconds. To a video of a man sat at a round glass garden table showing how best to pour a Guinness from a can. The grey-haired man wearing a fleece upturns the can four times before cracking it open and swirling it around a pint glass as he pours to try and get a better distribution.

Following those five videos, Shakil watched another 35 videos, before closing TikTok just before 2.36am. He's been on the app for less than 10 minutes.

But in those few minutes – frankly, even in a fraction of them, in just the first five videos he was delivered – TikTok had done a good job of identifying who he was and what interested him. 'I'm Muslim, interested in career tips, and love going to the beach,' Shakil says. 'The only thing that was different was the drinking tips.' As a Muslim, he doesn't drink alcohol. TikTok had plenty of practice to understand what interested Shakil: he had opened the app at least 1,539 times since first trying it in earnest on Christmas Day, 2019, and in that time its algorithms had been able to understand how he interacted with 37,756 videos he'd seen on the app before then. It knew what he liked and what he didn't like, and when he was most likely to want succour or entertainment; career advice or comedy.

That July day was Shakil's busiest day on TikTok. He logged on to TikTok 29 separate times in 24 hours, the second of which was mere minutes after he closed the app the first time. He opened the app at:

2.37am
2.49am
2.53am
3.05am and
3.13am.

He managed to get a couple of hours snatched sleep, before TikTok was once more open at 5.24am and 5.44am. When he awoke just after 8am, it was once more one of the first things he checked, and did so four times in the next 45 minutes. He had a spurt of viewing in several sessions between 10.20am and 10.45am, before getting to work. Two-and-a-half minutes before 5pm he snatched a quick glance at TikTok, and again as the clock struck 5pm. He was back at 9.32pm, 9.42pm (twice) and 10.08pm. At 11.38pm he reopened TikTok and watched 10 videos before going to bed – though at a little after 1am the next day he'd reopen the app.

In a single day, Shakil had watched 786 videos – three times the already hefty average of 264 TikToks he consumes every 24 hours. The other videos, beyond the pool, the drinking, the beauty blogger and the interview advice, give an insight into his interests and demonstrate the way to distract him. He was presented with videos about a bougie (high-class) apartment in Washington DC and its furniture fittings; the breaking of a land barrier by a giant digger, a torrent of water from a nearby lake pouring into a freshly dug hole; and impossibly beautiful people hanging out on a sailboat as the wind rattled the microphone on the mobile phone.

And of course, he was served, just before 10.36am, the requisite video of Charli D'Amelio, TikTok's biggest public face, in this case performing a carefully choreographed routine to Dababy's *Rockstar*, sashaying her hips and showing her lilac-painted fingernails.

The amount of time Shakil lingered on each video is also telling. Like most of us, when confronted by the power of nature or something awe inspiring – such as the video of extending the lake with the help of the mechanical teeth of a digger – he stops a little longer. Sometimes he watches it multiple times before scrolling on. He watches some videos, like ones where 26-year-old Mariah Amato saunters up to the camera and dances to a pop song in her bedroom while wearing grey sweatpants and a tight crop top, a little longer than the one where she teaches viewers the choreography of a popular dance on TikTok while wearing a billowy set of pyjamas. (Shakil wasted less than a second on that video before flicking on to the next one.)

Shakil is one of the most avid users I've encountered. Others use the app in moderation. Hollie Geraghty, a journalist from west London and professed TikTok fan, watched 2,142 videos in 250 days – around eight per day. Geraghty's relationship with TikTok is a little more complicated than that, though: she goes days, and sometimes weeks, without logging on, before bingeing, opening the app a dozen or more times a day. On 20 July 2020, for instance, she watched 132 videos in 13 different sessions on the app. That pales in comparison to her biggest binge, when she watched more than 300 videos over a 24-hour time period from around 11:30pm on 29 June to 11:30pm on 30 June, logging on 14 times.

The numbers demonstrate the level of information TikTok can collect on its users, and reinforce the strength of its algorithm to decide what interests people. Like a modern-day palm reader, it uses clues and cues to understand who we are and what we want to hear – or in this case, see. But unlike the sideshow charlatans, it doesn't have to dig for that information. We offer it readily. And that information helps TikTok build out its services, control our data, and improve the experience – better than any third-party company could ever dream of. TikTok likes to hold all the cards.

16
CONTROLLING
THE ECOSYSTEM

Business history is littered with examples of companies set up to service the needs of a thriving new industry. As the movie industry grew, for instance, the number of hangers-on at the Hollywood studio lots rose accordingly. Today, talent agents and casting directors meet in restaurants, agreeing roles for actors. Special effects houses, set designers, prop stores and caterers provide everything needed for production. The same is true in online industries: you can hire people to design your websites, market your companies, and secure you rankings at the top of Google searches. When YouTube first started becoming a putative industry with its own hierarchy of stars, a slew of hangers-on rushed into the market to offer their services.

In the late 2000s, a gold rush took place, where companies that called themselves multi-channel networks (MCNs) took a cut of a creator's income in return for acting as a talent agent, manager and deal broker. (In reality, the worst MCNs piled their influencers high, skimmed off profits, and offered little personalised support to their talent.) The industry settled down and broke out the supply chain into discrete parts. Talent agents managed brand deals and brokered agreements to hawk products. Managers juggled the chaotic schedule of a YouTuber on the rise, making sure they had time to record the videos that made money while holding off demanding fans and sifting through interview requests from journalists eager to learn the secrets of their success. Influencer marketing specialists connected established offline business brands with bright young online video creators – and took their fair share of a cut from any resulting deal. Lawyers specialised in drafting influencer deals, and keeping any brand deals brokered within advertising rules.

Scanning the YouTube ecosystem today, you'll see a whole world of hangers-on, movers and shakers, and big deal brokers – with varying degrees of professionalism and success. YouTube sustains an entire sector of business, as well as providing jobs for the creators who stand in front the camera.

TikTok is different. While elements of that industry still survive, with consultants who think they've found the secret to success on TikTok offering hopefuls the chance of supercharging their profiles, and managers shepherding talent through the fractious first stages of fame, ByteDance has decided that, in contrast to YouTube, it wants the opportunity to keep a larger slice of the pie for itself. Entire sectors of the influencer industry that are free to the open market when tied to other platforms like Instagram or YouTube are clasped tightly to TikTok.

Plenty of firms offer insights into the identity of the movers and shakers on the app, and who are the hot new creators to follow. But TikTok – in keeping with its Chinese background through ByteDance – wants to keep more of that ecosystem within the company's walls. 'It's the way Chinese companies work, and in the

West we just have to get used to the fact that certain companies are going to own the industry,' says Fabian Ouwehand, a Dutch entrepreneur who set up his company, UpLab, in China's Shenzhen in 2016. He quit his job in Singapore when he recognised there was an opportunity to capitalise on the strong growth of the new app called Douyin.

It's a smart business decision: by offering some of the services most useful to users of your app and the companies looking to advertise to them, you keep a larger share of revenue. It's a model that YouTube doesn't fully control in the same way: third parties often got there first, and brokered better brand deals, leaving YouTube reliant on taking a cut of advertising revenue alone from its biggest stars. But it does mean that the ability for enterprise is severely curtailed. Agents and talent brokers are still needed on TikTok, but it's more for the ability to do deals off the platform – a TV show appearance for a TikTok star, say – rather than anything on the app itself. If you're ByteDance, and you're able to control the selling of adverts, and the promotion of products within the app, you can keep the commission made on each and every one. In China, 60% of ByteDance's $27 billion in advertising revenue comes from Douyin alone. That's on top of the money ByteDance receives because it owns and runs the app on which all the content is being viewed. As far as double-dipping goes, it's not a bad deal.

You might think creators and advertisers would treat that with suspicion. After all, if the company that runs the app runs the market, there's nothing to stop it setting prices for talent that suits it, rather than the parties to each deal. It's a controlled economy, not a market economy. But TikTok can trade on prior precedent to persuade everyone involved of the benefits of its way of working things. For the best part of two decades, the nascent world of influencer marketing has struggled to shake off the bad reputation of its early snake oil salesmen, people who had the foresight to see the way in which the market was growing and try and make a few quick bucks. However, those early adopters didn't fully understand or appreciate the importance of making a long-term relationship, and often burned the talent and the advertisers they worked with. Early MCNs piled on the talent, building out improbably large rosters of creators all of whom they couldn't possibly provide with tailored advice and support. And as a result, standards slipped. The industry became known for shady practices. Influencers felt burned, and advertisers felt conned. What could have been a vibrant free market was tarnished by the greed of a few early adopters.

Influencer marketing hasn't ever really recovered since. It's been targeted by successive investigations from advertising standards authorities, principally in the US and UK, who highlight influencers who receive money to promote a product but don't declare it in their online posts. It's been leant on by regulators, and besmirched by the media. Companies who want to put money into influencer marketing know they have to do it in order to compete in the 21st century, but they appreciate that the market is such that they may end up wasting their money on some charlatans or misguided, mistargeted adverts. It's priced in to firm's budgets that they'll lose some money to inertia or incompetence, as if they were dealing with a kleptocratic country. In short, the market doesn't work properly.

Which may be why the TikTok Creator Marketplace was so warmly welcomed when it was launched in early 2020. The platform – a website that connects creators and brands with each other, allowing influencers to hawk their wares and companies to hawk their products – is a boon for both parties. Businesses wanting to promote a product, say a new phone or computer game, can search for creators with more than 10,000 followers based on a variety of different filters. You can look for people based in a certain country, or if they're in the United States, by state. You can search for sub-sections of the app, such as sports stars, beauty influencers or food creators. And you can, once you've spotted creators you may want to work with, then look at the demographics of their audience to decide whether it's a right fit for your brand. That can include the type of device they're using to access TikTok, as well as age, gender and location.

Once a brand has found a creator it would like to promote its product, the Creator Marketplace allows them to contact that person, and engage in a negotiation about how much it would be willing to pay to have the person mention their product in a video. From beginning to end, TikTok has theoretical oversight – which is just the way it wants it. And because of that oversight, brands and influencers can be convinced that the whole process is more legitimate than risking it out in the jungle of influencer marketing.

It's a smart decision that helps reassure all sides. ByteDance instigated it after seeing the issues Vine had with keeping its creators' content.

17
MANAGING
THE TALENT

Spies are famously recruited at university by a tap on the shoulder and some kind words. For TikTok stars of a similar age, an invitation to join the club of elite influencers given representation by talent management companies often comes through an Instagram direct message.

Twenty-year-old Noah Beck was a star soccer player, playing as a centre midfielder in his Utah school team, and ended up joining the Portland Pilots, the University of Portland's football team. He was offered a full sports scholarship by the university. But Portland wasn't just buying into a good footballer. As well as a versatile playmaker, Portland had recruited one of TikTok's rising names.

By then, Beck had built an audience in the millions on TikTok – the kind of numbers that get you noticed by companies like TalentX Entertainment, an agency that manages the interests of young would-be idols of social media. So the company came calling for Beck after assessing his viability as a potential investment.

The University of Portland, and the Pilots too, would probably have known the day was going to come. Barring a viral video of a flash mob in the middle of a basketball game that went crazy on YouTube in 2011, the sports team's YouTube presence was minimal. Just 2,000 people subscribe to its channel on the site, and most videos get hundreds of views. But a 98-second long introduction to Noah Beck, the football team's latest signing, had 690,000 views. It was clear Beck was destined for something apart from being a presence in the middle of the football pitch.

Some 89% of Beck's fans on TikTok are women, according to data TalentX Entertainment tracks through TikTok, shown to me in the middle of 2020. Four in 10 of them are from the United States, with his next popular groups of fans based in the United Kingdom, Brazil, Canada and Germany. In the last week of July 2020, he grew his audience by 1.1 million people. His average video on the app in the middle of 2020 was seen 6.3 million times, and a quarter of his audience was under the age of 18. He was, in the late spring of 2020, one of social media's fastest rising stars.

Beck gravitated around the group of TikTok creators represented by Lentz's company, TalentX Entertainment, which was set up by Josh Richards, one of Sway LA's biggest stars, as well as a businessman in his own right. Through one of the creators TalentX represents, the company learned about Beck's meteoric rise on apps like TikTok and Instagram in January. It gleaned that he had an abnormally high engagement rate – meaning people didn't just scroll past his content on social media platforms, but would like, comment and share it at an unheard-of frequency. At first, TalentX didn't bother trying to speak to him: 'He's on a full-ride soccer scholarship,' says Lentz. 'In the US, if you're an NCAA athlete, you're not able to do social media and make money. There was no point in us representing him.'

But as Beck's social media following swelled, he made it known he was thinking of leaving college and the scholarship behind and trying social media full-time.

When he came next to Los Angeles, Lentz and Mike Gruen, vice president of TalentX, took him out to dinner twice, spoke to his parents over Facetime, and talked Beck through the pros and cons of leaving behind tuition and a sports career for the fleeting fame of social media. 'We were very up front with him, saying: 'Look: you have a full-ride scholarship. You're also in a moment in time where you've grown faster than almost everyone else,' and we talked about how we could monetise him and grow his career.' Beck signed with TalentX in June 2020 and had completed seven brand deals within a month. He grew his Instagram following from 200,000 to 2.2 million, and his TikTok support similarly.

When Beck signed with TalentX he also joined Sway LA, one of the collaborative Hype Houses that popped up to capitalise on the growth of TikTok and to pool resources, talent and their resultant audiences together to maximise the drawing power of all those there. At first he didn't know any of the other people he now lives with in a luxury mansion in California, posting carefree videos to TikTok.

Lentz texted the members of Sway LA and laid out the reality of the situation: Beck was a hot commodity, with unparalleled social media success. Would they be interested in hanging out for a couple of days to see if they could click? Initially the response was lukewarm. 'The guys were like, "Oh, not sure",' says Lentz. Then they looked at his numbers. They saw how he was growing on TikTok – by himself: Beck didn't collaborate with any other TikTokers, and didn't piggyback on the reflected glory of other creators with different or bigger followers. They quickly changed their tune. Beck should come to stay the night.

The meeting went well. Beck joined Sway LA. Within nine days his Instagram following went from 200,000 to one million because of the connection to the established social media stars. As we spoke in late July 2020, Lentz was finalising a low six-figure deal for Beck that would see him endorse a brand with a handful of posts.

That was just the start, though. 'We want to build longstanding businesses, so that way our clients don't just pop off for a year then have it go away,' Lentz says.

For Beck, that means a five-point plan. It involves sponsorships, a merchandise range, business partnerships where he takes ownerships in companies that would be relevant to him, getting a YouTube channel set up from which he could make a monthly income from adverts presented alongside his videos, and landing acting roles in Hollywood – for which Lentz signed him up to acting classes three weeks before we spoke. The investment in Beck as a future star was significant: Lentz declined to say how much the company had spent on promoting him, but it appeared to be a lot.

In exchange, TalentX gets 20% of any income, and would expect Beck to hold up his half of the bargain. 'For him, it just centres around staying relevant, being consistent, posting content and being brand safe and not being too problematic, says Lentz. 'It's definitely an investment.'

That was challenged at the height of the summer, when Beck was one of a handful of creators criticised for hosting ostentatious birthday parties that brought dozens of influencers together into the same mega-mansions at a time when coronavirus was spreading across California. Beck in particular came under scrutiny when Bryce Hall, another TikToker and founding member of SwayLA, who has 20 million followers on the app, celebrated his 21st birthday. Video footage taken of the party, held in the Hollywood Hills, showed little social distancing, plenty of drinking, strippers wearing skimpy underwear grinding their bodies against the newly-of-age Hall – and a visit from the Los Angeles Police Department.

The police – who were initially indistinguishable from the male stripper wearing a police costume hired for the event – came to break up the party, the second time they'd visited the house on Hollywood's Appian Way, a street lined with multi-million dollar homes, in a week. Los Angeles' mayor threatened to cut off their power and water supply.

Hall, Beck and some of the others in Sway LA were seemingly unrepentant about their fun-loving during the time of an international pandemic. In videos later posted to TikTok, they poked fun at their more moralistic fans who warned them the electricity and water cuts could be imminent.

It was an ill-advised demonstration of bravado. The local mayor called a press conference shortly afterwards to announce he had instructed prosecutors to open an investigation into Hall and Grey for violating the city's party house ordinance. If they were found guilty and convicted, they could be imprisoned for a year and fined. While Beck managed to duck prosecution, he was instead tried in the court of public opinion: an attempt to 'cancel' him, by withdrawing his huge amounts of support, got underway, with people finding inappropriate posts he had liked, and highlighting mistruths he seemed to make about his footballing past – including that he had been offered a scholarship at the far more prestigious Yale University alongside Portland. It was an instructive moment for the young man: as quickly as your audience builds you up, they can also take you down a peg or two.

The controversy passed. Beck remains a bad boy on TikTok – not that that's bad for business. As this book went to press a year later, he had grown his audience to 27.5 million fans.

18
SUPPORTING
THE COMMUNITY

As well as spending handsomely to attract users to the platform, TikTok has nurtured and valued the opinions of key leaders within the community since its early days. ByteDance has been supporting some of its creators on Douyin in China through direct financial support, employing them almost as contracted beta testers and advocates for some of its new features. It's the kind of scheme that influencer marketing boss Fabian Ouwehand's girlfriend found herself on when she joined Douyin in its early days. But, as we'll discover, while the company was more than happy big bucks to pay celebrities like Cardi B to start posting on the app, it took TikTok two years from its official launch in the West to start supporting its creators in the way Alex Zhu foresaw for Musical.ly.

In those two years, TikTok had become enormous. It had grown from 55 million monthly active users in January 2018 to 732 million in October 2020. Some of those creators had become bona fide stars of their own, inking television deals, gaining representation from Hollywood talent agencies, and bringing out books that extended their brand beyond the borders of TikTok. A Vine-like rebellion was brewing, if TikTok didn't give its talent base the ability to start earning a crust. So it did.

The TikTok Creator Fund was rolled out first in the United States, with the promise of $1 billion of investment between 2020 and 2022. A further $300 million was earmarked for creators in Europe, with other countries likely to follow in due course. It was a gamechanger for those who had managed to build fame, but not fortune, on TikTok.

Curtis Newbill is a 24-year-old whose family moved between Rio Rancho, New Mexico and Lutz, Florida when he was a child. Like many digital creators, he started out on YouTube, posting comedy videos, before finding a more natural home on TikTok. He's now firmly in the app's upper echelons. Though hard data doesn't exist, he reckons that his 100 to 300 million views a month puts him in the top 50 TikTokers in the United States. He's friends with the D'Amelio sisters, queens of the app, and also hangs around with talent from both the Hype House and Sway LA. In short, he's connected. And he's popular: seven million people follow the bleached blond, bright-teethed star as he posts comedy skits and clowns about in front of camera with his beautiful, famous friends.

Newbill had eagerly been anticipating the opportunity to cash in on his then-five million-strong following the moment he heard about the Creator Fund. 'This should've been something that was implemented day one,' he told me. He, and others, were beginning to grow a little frustrated by the seeming imbalance in the arrangement between them and the app – and it echoed the concerns Vine's biggest stars had a few years earlier. 'Right now creators virtually get absolutely northing for bringing traction to the app,' he explained. But he had been excited by the idea that things were changing, and financial support was coming from TikTok that would recognise his talent and what he brought to TikTok.

A billion dollars sounds like a large amount – it is a large amount – but when you're talking about a userbase of hundreds of millions worldwide, it becomes much smaller. Not everyone was eligible for the cash: you had to be over 18 (discounting a significant proportion of TikTok's users), and have a following of more than 10,000 people who watched your videos 10,000 times or more in a given month. But in Europe, for instance, TikTok was forecasting tens of thousands of people would have the opportunity to get some share of the $300 million they planned to disburse over the course of three years there. Which is why it perhaps wasn't surprising when the first sign-ups to the Creator Fund got their first payment notifications through, and realised that for many it wouldn't buy them lunch.

Dozens of creators shared their earnings with me, some incredulous and many deflated. Where they were expecting a small fortune, they instead got an average of around three cents per 1,000 views. Newbill – one of TikTok's bona fide superstars – got around half that. An even bigger female friend of his ended up with an average of 1.2 cents per thousand eyeballs, he had calculated. The first day he was eligible, people watched Newbill's videos 3.8 million times. For that he received $60.22. He was trying to rationalise why the number seemed so low. Could it be because he had a large proportion of international viewers, who perhaps couldn't be monetised by TikTok through adverts? No, he showed me his demographics, which showed that his biggest base was in the United States. He was hugely disappointed.

A few days later, I checked in with him. He was now in two minds. 'On one hand, at least we are getting something, but on the other hand getting a penny per thousand views almost seems insulting,' he said. The amount he'd earn from those views – between $2,000 and $6,000 a month – may seem like a lot to the average American, but he was living in Los Angeles and maintaining the lifestyle of the top TikTok creator he was. 'It makes me feel even more so for the average creator who's working really hard, trying to grow their audience and spend time on their TikToks, just to be getting paid pennies for their efforts,' he lamented. TikTok had been saying for two years it was working on a way to add stability for creators looking to earn a living, but the fund didn't change a thing, he reckoned.

Despite learning some of the lessons of Vine, TikTok may need to tweak the rewards on offer to its creators to keep them happy, though its increasing dominance is hard to challenge.

19
EXTRA MONEY
FOR STARS

From the first interview I conducted with Alex Zhu back in 2016, before Musical.ly was bought by ByteDance, TikTok's users had tended to be younger than the average social media user. But there are only a finite number of teenagers around the world who can be convinced to clown around on camera. At some point, the app needed to start expanding its userbase beyond them in order to guarantee untrammelled, perpetual growth.

Rich Waterworth, a former YouTube executive who had spent 10 years at the Google-owned video platform before jumping over to TikTok 12 days before Christmas, knew that well. 2019 had been an extraordinary year for TikTok, he told me in late December, but it wanted to expand its horizons. He brought up the example of a 61-year-old farmer from Wiltshire called Chris Franklin, who runs Caenhill Countryside Centre, a charity that connects children with farm animals in order to educate them about the world.

I had heard Franklin's name before: he was a stock character the company rolled out to show the expansiveness of its userbase and was first mentioned to me in a call that summer. It only took a few minutes using the app to recognise that Franklin was an outlier when confronted by a sea of impossibly young, attractive faces. But six months down the line, things were changing.

For sure, TikTok was still seeing tremendous growth in its core category of young people. Waterworth, like any tech executive, wasn't willing to share specifics, but was willing to confess that the company was seeing really fast growth among users aged between 16 and 24. Like any good journalist, I got the data anyway. By the summer of 2020, internal slides distributed by TikTok to advertisers showed that 39% of TikTok's 17 million monthly active users in the UK were aged between 18 and 24. A further quarter were 25 to 34. 'We've had loads of parents coming onto the platform and older, millennials-plus, coming onto the platform, to change their perception of what the platform is,' said Yazmin How, TikTok's UK editorial head honcho. 'They thought it was just lipsyncing or dancing. But as the userbase has diversified, we've seen the content has followed. They've started creating the content they like consuming.'

The reality is that the users are often younger, but because of rules banning advertising to children, TikTok executives were far less frank about that in 2020 than the Musical.ly co-founder of 2016, who readily admitted users as young as 13. The coyness about the age of users was the result of a pair of fines in less than nine months. In February 2019, TikTok was fined $5.7 million because its acquisition, Musical.ly, had breached American rules protecting children from undue data collection online. The US Federal Trade Commission (FTC), which levied the fine, claimed that Musical.ly's owners 'knew many children were using the app but they still failed to seek parental consent before collecting names, email addresses, and other personal information from users under the age of 13.'

Another fine didn't affect TikTok or ByteDance, but its ramifications were felt by every app popular with children. In September 2019, the FTC struck again. YouTube reached a settlement with regulators for violating the same rules protecting children online and agreed to pay a $170 million fine. It was 'an important milestone' for all social platforms who had child users, said Dylan Collins, chief executive of a company focused on online child safety.

Then in December 2019, TikTok was subject to a lawsuit alleging it had collected data from kids under the age of 13 without explicit consent – claims the company denies. However, leaked internal data shows one in four of TikTok's users are aged between 13 and 17. A further 42% were under the age of 24. Just 15% of users who logged onto the app in March 2019 were aged 35 and over.

The young users keep TikTok vibrant, but they also cause a headache for the app's owners. So TikTok wanted to expand: TikTok had seen fast growth in those aged 25 to 34, and even older, Waterworth told me. 'TikTok is really getting very broad in terms of the content being shared there and in terms of the type of creators and users we see.'

TikTok planned to capitalise on that by spending big on a traditional Christmas advertising campaign on television and billboards featuring David Beckham and pop star Lewis Capaldi, drawing in people by saturating the airwaves with information about the app at the same time as young relatives pestered them to appear in their own TikToks while together at Christmas. (It's a well-worn strategy within TikTok: the app's parent company spent up to $3 million a day on advertising in the United States in 2019 alone.)

But the glitzy TV ad campaign, which involved people jumping in and out of a neon frame lit up in the blue and red colours of the TikTok logo, almost didn't happen. The 200 kilogram wooden box containing the frame for the campaign was delivered to the lobby of TikTok's shared WeWork shared office space in Holborn, London. And it would only go up the stairs. Around a dozen of the company's workers ended up heaving it up three storeys.

Those employees were well paid. TikTok's pursuit of world dominance doesn't come cheap, and as well as hard-earned users through an engaging product, the company is also paying to play in many ways. It's not just the wall-to-wall sponsorship of key parts of the landscape at events like VidCon where you can see the money being splurged, or the television advertising campaigns featuring chart-topping pop stars and celebrities. In the world of tech startups where salaries are already inflated, TikTok is paying top dollar to coax workers from such competitors as Facebook and YouTube. A machine learning engineer at TikTok could earn £200,000, overseeing a team of 10 staff. Many seem to have joined: TikTok has managed to sweep up many of tech's big names, recruiting staff from YouTube and other platforms such as Yahoo.

TikTok has also hired from a number of different industries. Much of the marketing team are former journalists, swept up by the firm just as their previous employers cut jobs back to the bone. Two were even poached from the office of the former leader of the Liberal Democrats, Britain's third political party, to join the company, while TikTok's director of government relations and public policy, Theo Bertram, is a former adviser to two British prime ministers. The company, at the time thinking of basing its international arm in London, was hiring big there, and in Dublin, where it announced a $500 million trust and safety centre to handle all its European data. Fifteen percent of all the job vacancies listed on TikTok's website in mid-2020 were based in those two offices.

The spending extends to talent, too. Unlike the Creator Fund, which is available to rank and file users, TikTok is willing to splash the cash if it thinks you'll bring new eyeballs and users to the app. Celebrity endorsements don't come cheap, and TikTok has been willing to offer money to creators on other platforms to set up accounts on TikTok. A casting call from TikTok, disseminated through influencer marketing agencies, asked for American-based comedians, gamers, DIY influencer and pet creators who were already on YouTube or Instagram to come and join TikTok and begin posting content. For creating an account, TikTok would give them $500. For every video they posted after that according to a weekly schedule, they'd receive $25. TikTok expected them to post three original videos a week for eight weeks, each one between 11 and 16 seconds long. Influencers weren't allowed to mention any of their other social media accounts in the caption or the video, and had to include the hashtag #TikTokPartner.

Complete the request and the influencer would receive $1,100 into their bank account. For every video that hit 100,000 views they would get an extra $200, rising to $300 for every 200,000 views and $500 for a million-plus views.

You may be wondering how many people took up TikTok on that offer. While not every single post tagged with #TikTokPartner is an official influencer post, nearly 135,000 videos have used the hashtag, and have been seen nearly 7.8 billion times. The average video using that hashtag has been seen around 58,000 times, according to data gathered using Pentos, a TikTok analytics tool.

For influencers with large followings who could meet those bonus targets, it was theoretically possible to earn $13,100 for posting four and a half minutes of footage to the app. Larger carrots were dangled in front of other influencers. In December 2018, a number of influencers were contacted by an influencer marketing agency and asked to start posting content to TikTok. In exchange, they'd receive up to $500 and could earn a $5,000 bonus dependent on performance.

Similar documents shared around the influencer industry in India suggested that thousands of creators in the country were on contracts that paid them not just to post on TikTok, but also to share the content more widely through a 'forwarding clips commitment' clause. Creators could reportedly earn anything from $250 to $1,750 per month, depending on their popularity on the platform – a veritable bounty in a country where the average monthly wage is around $425.

Not bad work if you can get it, even though that's a pittance compared to the amount TikTok is rumoured to have paid at least one Instagram influencer to hawk its product. According to the Wall Street Journal, ByteDance forked out more than $1 million for the unnamed influencer to promote a single video.

'That's actually a very common strategy in China,' says Fabian Ouwehand. Ouwehand knows better than most that this is a common way to lure creators to platforms in China. Not only has he been monitoring how ByteDance has grown the two parallel short-form video apps it now runs around the world, his partner Erin was one of the first creators on Douyin – ever.

'She got paid for it,' he explains. 'Quite a bit of money.' In 2016, soon after Douyin had launched as A.me, Ouwehand's girlfriend was contacted by a ByteDance representative. She was one of around 20 or 30 creators that the company approached who had built a base on other platforms. Ironically, ByteDance was looking to poach Ouwehand's partner from Musical.ly, the app it would end up buying just over a year later. The offer was straightforward:

join A.me, post content and she'd receive around 300 Chinese yuan (RMB) for every video she posted, capped at a maximum of 4,000 RMB per month. That amount – equivalent at the time to around $600 – was roughly the same as a starting salary in China. 'It's pretty high,' says Ouwehand. 'They basically got that for making a few videos a month.' And that amount differed depending on a person's fame: others received more.

Ouwehand's partner, along with many others, took the money and became more than a creator: she was a collaborator. For two years, she worked alongside the company, creating content – in the end, exclusively as the company demanded more from creators on the payroll – while also helping provide feedback on how to develop the app. It's a practice that continues today: one American TikTok user I spoke to was approached in March 2021 through a message on his app, inviting him to join a beta testing group. He'd be given access to a test version of the app where TikTok would explore ideas for new features, and he'd be asked to participate in a Facebook group offering feedback on the ideas – all under a non-disclosure agreement, of course.

Paying top creators to become beta testers, and to provide real-time suggestions on how to improve the app while also growing the platform at the same time, isn't cheap. If every one of the A.me launch creators was paid $600 a month, ByteDance was spending at least $144,000 a year on its early creative team. But as with the $1 million dangled in front of a big Instagrammer to make the leap, TikTok can recoup the outlay by charging brands to advertise. As of June 2020, placing an 'in-feed ad' – a short snippet of footage that appears in the endless scroll of videos – cost a minimum of $25,000 for a maximum 15-second video. That's a cool $1,667 per second. If you want an even more prime position, the video that plays when users open up the app, it'd cost between $210,000 and $240,000. A hashtag challenge – quirky actions users mimic and post underneath a specific hashtag – starts at $175,000.

And the creators joining the platform can earn, too. One service, Artist Influence, offers to act as a broker between record labels and TikTok influencers, who could use the music in a video. 'The network operates by posting content specific to each influencers' niche while utilizing your music in their content,' the company claims. 'The music is pushed to the influencers' highly engaged audiences through a piece of their organic content, resulting in highly-engaged click-throughs.' It's never made clear whether the videos would be flagged as an advert, given that money changes hands during the process. Your music reaching one million people on TikTok would cost $350. Reaching five million costs $1,600. To reach 20 million, $4,800. The company providing the service claims to have worked with the likes of Warner Records, Sony Music, Universal Music Group and Live Nation.

CREATOR FOCUS
CUMBERMATCH

Name: Peter Clarke
Username: @cumbermatch
Following: 347
Followers: 2.8M
Likes: 24.2M
Speciality: Looking like Benedict Cumberbatch

The offices of the *Financial Times* in London might not seem like an auspicious place to give birth to the career of a TikTok star, but then again, very little is normal about the career trajectory of Peter Clarke.

The 43-year-old business analyst was working as a contractor for the *Financial Times* in spring 2019, stuck at a desk in a large, low-ceilinged open plan office that was like a time capsule from the 1980s. In the dim light, his jovial colleagues recognised his uncanny resemblance to the Hollywood A-lister Benedict Cumberbatch. It was something Clarke got a lot: people would always mention his passing resemblance to the actor, but he never really saw it – until he donned the costume of Doctor Strange, Cumberbatch's character in the Marvel Cinematic Universe, at a party and took a handful of photos on his phone.

Those photos ended up being passed around the *Financial Times* office, and Clarke was gently cajoled into posting them on Instagram, with a colleague suggesting he set up a new account called 'Cumber-match' based on his resemblance to the star. Quickly, the photos gained momentum, with users lapping up the slightly skew-whiff lookalike.

But the people logging onto Clarke's Cumbermatch profile weren't content with still images. They wanted to see how he compared to their idol in action. They suggested he join a relatively new video sharing app called TikTok. A fellow accidental lookalike celebrity, a former community college computer operator called Itzhak Hershkovich, who had managed to make a living out of his eerie resemblance to Robert Downey Jr under the username NYTonyStark, also recommended he give it a go. Hershkovich even offered to help Clarke out by encouraging him to duet some of his videos – a way to piggyback on the success of another creator's pre-existing audience.

Cumbermatch on TikTok was born. 'It all happened quite quickly,' Clarke admits when I spoke to him more than a year later, in July 2020. He had managed to build up a large fanbase – 1.4 million people, by that point, and was starting to develop a significant following. Clarke had found his groove on the platform. After the duets, he'd started off mouthing key moments of dialogue from Benedict Cumberbatch's biggest shows and television programmes in a crude attempt at lip syncing, but found they didn't really hit home with viewers. Instead what they loved was seeing the inscrutable Hollywood star – or someone who looked an awful lot like him – doing things that he'd never ordinarily do, like interacting with the audience, or performing comedy skits the real-life star wouldn't dare partake in. 'Usually it's the least expected TikTok that gets the recognition and gets the likes and views,' he says.

Clarke isn't the only lookalike thriving on the app. As with many things on the app, there is a whole subculture of people who have managed to build a following because of their resemblance – passing or otherwise – to celebrities. Paige Niemann, a 17-year-old who looks like the pop singer Ariana Grande when she applies a thick lip of makeup and winged eyeliner, has managed to parlay that into a following of 10.5

million. With it, some reckon she's also drawn the ire of the person she looks like. Grande has previously posted comments attacking looka-likes that many have construed as being aimed at Niemann. Grande said she didn't understand why people think 'ponytail TikTok girls who think doing the Cat Valentine voice and wearing winged eyeliner and a sweatshirt is doing a good impersonation of me'. Niemann responded that's why she's no longer a fan of the singer.

Other impersonators remain fans of the people they're claiming to look like. Priscila Beatrice, a 29-year-old from Brazil, used to get regular comments from friends saying she looked like the Bahamian pop star Rihanna. Like Clarke, she was cajoled into joining TikTok, signing up in March 2020, after six years of a career as Rihanna's 'official double in Brazil.' She gained half a million followers in five months – many of them because of the similarity she has with Rihanna. 'On TikTok I play with the image,' she says. 'My followers love it when I do it. In real life, it's amazing, because I can see in the eyes of Rihanna fans all the love they feel – it's surreal.'

But while overnight success may seem simple to some of those who have managed to build up an audience for looking like others, TikTok fame isn't easy to achieve. Up until the coronavirus crisis, when Clarke took the decision with his wife to stay at home and look after the chil-dren, he was juggling being an itinerant business analyst with looking after two children and his career as an online entertainer. 'Finding the time to do it is very difficult,' he admits. Once a week, after the kids are in bed on a Thursday evening, Clarke will take himself away from the family and start planning and recording videos to release for the next week.

The arrangement puts him at a disadvantage compared to others on TikTok. The platform thrives on trends, and pre-planning and filming content to be released on a drip feed throughout the week sometimes means he ends up behind the curve on the app's biggest shifts. However, he's still popular with his audience, and increasingly popular with advertisers. In the months before we spoke, a number of them had approached Clarke asking if he'd be willing to advertise their products in videos. 'It's not a great deal, and it's certainly not enough to make a career out of it,' he says. 'But I am getting more and more people asking me to do paid posts.' It was making him reconsider what would happen after the coronavirus crisis abated. 'You never know – I might not go back to being a business analyst at the end of this.'

PART IV

INSIDE BYTEDANCE

20
YIMING
ZHANG'S CREATION

ByteDance is open, independent, and driven – just like its founder. Its ambition is evident from its location: in inner Beijing. If you want to know the standing of a company in the Chinese capital, look where its offices are. A sprawling city with 2 million inhabitants isn't kind to commuters. Its rush hour begins at 5am – all because the average commute to work across the city is 26 kilometres, or 16 miles. Snarled up in rush hour traffic, or crammed into commuter line trains, it can take two hours for a typical employee to reach their workplace and return home. Some travel for six hours a day.

Being closer to the city centre, which has the best commuter connections, is a boon. And ByteDance's Beijing headquarters are pretty close to the centre of the Chinese capital – lying partway between the third and fourth ring roads that radiate out from the hub of the city centre. Of course, cutting down on commuting time to the city centre if you're stuck out in the sticks costs money – which is why the ByteDance salary, which is by some accounts far higher than any other tech company in China, helps ease the transition. You can simply afford to live closer to the city centre.

ByteDance is known for paying the highest salaries in China's tech sector. While most tech companies offer you a little more than you were paid at the last job you held, ByteDance looks at the current market dynamics and gives you that – which results in huge salary inflations (there is also the opportunity to earn eight times your annual salary through good performance bonuses). Through competitive salaries, just as it has in the West, ByteDance managed to lure many workers from China's pre-existing tech giants, like Tencent and Baidu. Many were offered promotions and the chance to manage teams on top of a salary enhancement. In 2017, it even offered stock options – a tempting and potentially lucrative lure for those willing to bet on the company's runaway success. (Today, the stock option offer has been stripped back to senior employees.) Like Google, Facebook and other Silicon Valley firms, employees at ByteDance are given three square meals a day, and allowed to graze on snacks whenever they want. The food is said to be delicious.

Its openness stems from the 'ByteStyle principles' that are imbued through all employees – a crucial part of the company's DNA. Workers and managers are asked to encourage participation from everyone, and seek out views that challenge their own; they're asked to find the best solutions by widening their perspective; to 'take ownership, assume risks and break the mould,' and approach problems with the big picture in mind. They're also asked to dare to share honest opinions, and to avoid 'leader-pleasing.'

While Chinese business is intensely formal, with employees calling each other by titles such as 'teacher' if they've learned something from a colleague, Zhang wants you to call him by his name.

And not his surname. He likes 'Yiming'. That's it. In a culture, and a business world dominated by tiers and structure, Zhang built ByteDance to be a place where everyone is almost equal.

One employee who started at the company's Beijing offices in April 2019 and still works there today was amazed at the speed of the work, and the flatness of the hierarchy. It's possible, using Lark, the in-house work communications system developed by ByteDance that has since become a public-facing app, to find anyone in the company and directly communicate with them. You can privately message Yiming Zhang himself if you wish.

'It's a really open atmosphere, working in this company,' the employee said. 'We do have leaders, but I feel mostly that the leaders really want to listen to your opinions.' (As we'll see in later chapters, not everyone shares that view.)

That openness extends to dealing with outsiders. Though ByteDance has been buffeted by criticism from politicians far more strident than many of its predecessors, it's survived in better condition than most companies that have been the personal targets of the world's most powerful man. It proactively courts the press, where YouTube is often standoffish. I managed to speak to TikTok's managing director in the UK at four hours' notice two days before Christmas in 2019. It took several requests over the course of many years – and many refusals in the interim – to end up arranging an interview with YouTube's equivalent executive.

ByteDance is also independent-minded, despite the constraints of Chinese society. As could be seen in its assessment of short-form video apps before it launched TikTok, it does not just accept existing ways of doing things, but probes and challenges. Zhang is avowedly not a member of the communist party – a prerequisite for many Chinese tech executives. Huawei's boss,

Ren Zhengfei, spent nine years in the People's Liberation Army engineering corps in the 1970s and 80s.

ByteDance is driven by a ferocious work ethic. ByteDance may be different in many ways from other Chinese firms, but it fully ascribes to the national ethos of 9-9-6, working 9am to 9pm, six days a week. Employee rostering systems at ByteDance work in such a way that staff in China are expected to work every other Saturday. 'It's really hard work,' one employee explains. 'For the last year I've worked 12 hours a day, except for the weekend. For some people, working there for half a year or one year is fine, but two or three years is really hard.' (The taxi subsidy that ByteDance offers employees to get home if they end up working after 10pm is a sop to the tough working environment.) It's little wonder, then, that ByteDance churns through employees at a prodigious rate. For the vast numbers it regularly hires to join the company as fresh-faced new arrivals – around 1,200 jobs are listed at any one time on its website – there are a steady stream of ex-ByteDancers re-entering the job market and looking for a more casual pace of life, albeit with the cultural and career cachet of experience at one of the world's hottest tech companies on their CV.

In part that's down to the way that Zhang adopted the most productive elements of the Western way of work, and the most productive of the Chinese way, too. Alongside the 9-9-6 core, ByteDance also borrows from the target-heavy business ethos of OKR (objectives and key results). Popularised by Google and brought to ByteDance in its second year of operation, you're set targets every two months and expected to meet them – at which point, you're set a whole new set of goals. The hamster wheel has to keep spinning, and employees can't step off. It can be confusing at the best of times, and not everyone survives. One worker thrown headlong into big projects in the UK office left after a matter of weeks, feeling like nothing was explained to them and they were given unrealistic targets nonetheless.

Zhang's obsession with Google has led to ByteDance adopting other practices at its Beijing offices. Posters on the wall show motivational phrases from books about Facebook including 'Leaders start things,' *Shoe Dog*, the autobiography of Phil Knight founder of Nike, and *Trillion Dollar Coach* by Eric Schmidt, Google's former chief executive. Zhang convenes bi-monthly town hall meetings with his staff, borrowed too from Google. He's also eager to understand context from his users: as well as training his AI algorithm to ascertain what TikTok users want, he makes sure that those he employs use the app themselves. TikTok employees are actively encouraged to create accounts on the platform and post videos; in the past, he's even set targets for them to reach a certain number of likes, and make them do push-ups if they don't reach the goal. (The app's AI is seen as so powerful that in public-facing interviews between staff, employees are asked to describe the types of videos they encounter on their For You page as a way of learning more about the person.)

ByteDance sums up its ethos as 'context over control.' By that, Zhang means that he doesn't want to micromanage every single decision, but rather wants individual staff to feel like they can make decisions, based on informed data that the company sweeps up from its users. Rank and file employees, should they feel empowered by the data, can delve into developing a product or a feature without much oversight, if they think it has potential. It's designed to maximise innovation, and is done with the full knowledge that a good number of the ideas will fail. But some of them work, and become main products in the ByteDance roster. Several employees say this creates a spontaneity in the company. Others say it creates chaos and a sense of rudderless action: you either hold on to the runaway boulder coming down the track and try and make sense of why you're doing it later on when things calm down, or it crushes you.

Certainly, some of those I've spoken to have found working for a Chinese-based company, where many of the key decision makers remain rooted in China, difficult. One employee in the London office, whose team is split half and half between the UK and China, said working with Chinese staff can be complicated because of the language barrier, and their team planned to disconnect further from the head office in Beijing. Another in the US said it was normal to receive messages from Chinese colleagues through Lark, ByteDance's internal messaging system, at two or three in the morning. 'There's no concept of work-life balance at all,' they said. They also felt the level of interaction with and control from China was underplayed when they joined the company. 'Overall, I'd say TikTok is still very much China-driven.' They planned to leave the firm in the summer of 2021, after their annual bonus hit their bank account, and said they weren't the only one.

Scroll through Glassdoor, the website where employees rate their employers anonymously, and you'll first spot that satisfaction with TikTok is generally high. Four in 10 workers recommend joining the company to their friends. But dig deeper, and you start to see the cracks. Seemingly the hiring process isn't all that friendly. Reviews of the company's interviewing process are littered with complaints about the way it fishes for information about competitors from those who already work there, and treats potential hires rudely. Those who make it to the firm say that their experiences are mixed. One talks about being locked inside 'a Chinese prison'; another recommends the firm 'stop pretending it's a US-style company when it's Chinese.'

It is a Chinese company that wants to grow all over the world.

21
GROWING PAINS

ByteDance achieves expansion abroad by attaching the engine of its coding centre in Beijing to the wheels of foreign countries. While the engine is extremely powerful, sometimes the wheels can go in different directions, to the frustration of both Beijing and staff in outposts of Yiming Zhang's empire.

In all, ByteDance now has offices in 126 different cities worldwide, housing a total of 100,000 employees. In the early days when ByteDance is establishing a base in a country, the majority of the decision makers are Chinese, and from the company's core collection of executives. Slowly, as the firm tries to gain a foothold in the chosen country, it starts to hire people in power from the country themselves – partly a way of ensuring there's a long-lasting presence in each territory, but probably also as a useful defence against overzealous politicians' fears of a Chinese invasion.

The companies ByteDance runs are structured similarly, with regional and national hubs. Head over to its website and you can see a simplified company structure, showing how and where the power lies. At the head of everything is ByteDance Ltd, a Cayman Islands company. (If all ByteDance's 100,000 employees worked there, Caymans would have to build a lot more infrastructure. When one *New York Times* reporter asked how many people worked in the 264-square kilometre tax haven, a ByteDance spokesperson couldn't say.)

Underneath it lies ByteDance (HK) Limited, based in Hong Kong, which nominally oversees all the main China operating entities of its apps. Then there's TikTok Ltd, also based in the Cayman Islands, which controls separate companies that run the company's flagship app outside China. Two are in the US – a limited liability company that runs TikTok, and ByteDance Inc, which manages its other apps – and three elsewhere. TikTok KK looks after the app in Japan; TikTok Pte Ltd in Singapore oversees it in south-east Asia, and TikTok Information Technologies UK Ltd, registered in London, acts as the company's European base.

Staff in Beijing are constantly reminded that they are engaged in an international endeavour. ByteDance employees based in the company's Chinese headquarters have a group chat where they're fed videos made by users on TikTok outside China. A stream of videos from the US, the UK, Brazil and Vietnam fill up the screen, a reminder that they're not just developing the app for users in their own country. Zhang told reporters: 'It makes you realise that the world is a very big place, and it expands your horizons.'

In keeping with his international interests and ambition, Zhang doesn't languish in ByteDance HQ in Beijing. Two out of every three days in 2019, he spent on the road, travelling around the world. He's been said to be a particular fan of ducking into museums wherever he visits and taking in the exhibits, and enjoys musicals in London's West End. When he visits India, he spends time in the Dilli Haat market in Delhi, perusing its stalls selling handcrafted items from each state around India, in an attempt to understand the market and what the people there want. As part of the European expansion of TikTok, he bunked up in a friend's apartment in Paris and wandered its streets to try and comprehend its culture. In a letter to staff marking the company's eighth anniversary in March 2020, he said he would strive to visit every area that ByteDance had an office in the next three years 'to understand the company and learn the local culture.' Before the coronavirus shut down the world, Zhang planned to travel even more in 2020, telling journalists that schlepping through airport terminals and into uncharted territory was a way to 'understand more context.'

Staff overseas are encouraged to adopt the company's openness and ambition – but independence was harder to achieve when so much work remained in the Beijing engine.

One former ByteDance employee based in the United States with extensive experience in influencer marketing struggled with a company-wide system that seemed to give them autonomy to chart their own course, while in reality having to report to a Chinese team that ran in parallel with their US-based one.

'It was a lot of banging heads on walls,' they say. Their team – which brought influencers over to TopBuzz, the US equivalent of Toutiao – was led by an American manager. This manager technically also oversaw the equivalent team in China that developed new features for the app. ByteDance keeps much of its engineering team at headquarters in Beijing, and the coders are shared within departments. The so-called 'middle office' will work on different apps simultaneously, rolling out shared features that will work on all of them. 'You want to use the resource and do the work more effectively,' says one current ByteDance employee. (It's partly the reason why the equivalent apps, like TikTok outside China and Douyin inside the country, look so similar.) Yet the Chinese team, perhaps because of its proximity to top brass in Beijing, would often make direct representations over the head of the US-based boss. In the end, the TopBuzz boss gave up and let his underlings in Beijing make the decisions.

There was also friction based on the attempt to replicate exactly Toutiao's success in China in the United States with TopBuzz, without realising the differences in the market. At one point, the former employee's boss visited the Beijing offices and was proudly shown a wall full of framed pictures of influencers who had risen to fame on Toutiao. A number of them were pig farmers, a fixation of the firm. The US employee was expected to find their own equivalent for the US market, without much luck. 'There was just a disconnect between the way the influencer landscape was set up here versus there,' they say. Not that the team didn't try: the TopBuzz team in the US was given an annual budget of $3.5 million to spend on influencer acquisition for the app. Creators who would post content on the news-based app would be given $500 or $1,000 a month simply to show up, with performance bonuses based on the views their content gained that could rake in thousands of dollars.

After work and in the ByteDance cafeteria in Los Angeles, the former employee and their colleagues, many of whom were working on TikTok's US expansion, shared war stories of being overruled or not understood by Chinese colleagues.

22
FLEXING CELEBRITY
WITH ARNIE

A little sprinkle of stardust can go a long way, as the owners of restaurants and takeaways who like to hang poorly framed pictures of their famous patrons on the walls of their venues will tell you. The morning of 16 March 2019 was a momentous one for TikTok in the United States. And it was thanks to a fading film star turned politician best known for his muscles and robotic acting skills that the team at TikTok's Los Angeles offices had reason to celebrate.

That morning, employees at the company had opened up the app to be confronted by the sight of Arnold Schwarzenegger doing bicep curls on a machine in his home gym to the sound of *It's Raining Men* by The Weather Girls. The video, which saw the ageing Hollywood action icon jutting out his chin as he lifted the weights to his face, and eventually turning to the camera and raising an arched eyebrow, was a fillip – and a sign of supremacy for the app. TikTok had made it.

Schwarzenegger was an unusual TikToker. He was a few months away from his 72nd birthday – far older than the average user. He was a former politician, and a Hollywood star, who would ordinarily avoid joining social media platforms. It was, says an employee working at TikTok at the time said, the first 'true organic victory' the app had scored in the United States. Better yet, the former Californian governor had signed up of his own volition. For a company that was happy to throw money at people to join them, whether in their offices or in front of the camera lens, this was a major moment.

It signalled that TikTok had gained its own momentum, and the exit velocity was big enough that it could break out of its own controlled, artificial growth pattern. For someone like Schwarzenegger to not only be aware of the existence of TikTok, but also to feel compelled to go to the trouble of downloading the app, signing up and then posting his own videos, it was a big deal. The team were overjoyed. 'He just decided to do it and have fun,' says one former employee. 'It was the first time where we didn't have to manufacture everything. We didn't have to go and pitch PR about what a person was doing on TikTok or anything. It's like, one day we woke up, Arnold Schwarzenegger posted a TikTok, and you get a bunch of stories saying things like: "Arnold Schwarzenegger just broke the internet, check out this new app".'

It was vindication for the American-based team, who had been fighting a losing battle with their Chinese counterparts who wanted to try increasingly odd ways to attract users – at one point, a sweepstake was tabled. It was also a far cry from some of the previous attempts the app had made to recruit mainstream celebrities, and better yet, cost them nothing.

For everything Arnold Schwarzenegger did to be considered TikTok royalty by its American employees, American rapper, bona fide chart-topper and former stripper Cardi B did the opposite.

It took time, effort and a lot of money to convince Cardi B to join the platform. The app threw an amount believed to be in the high six figures for her to post to TikTok in January 2018, and while she did post videos, the results were underwhelming.

That wasn't necessarily the singer's fault. The contract she signed was a simple one, according to those with knowledge of it. She'd get a boatload of money for posting to the app, and there were very few constraints on the type of content she had to do. There weren't any parameters set about when she should post, or what she should post – or even how the videos should interact with her other social media platforms. It was all driven by the marketing department in Beijing who simply wanted a big star to make a splash. It seemingly didn't matter to the marketing department in Beijing – or something they hadn't considered – that Cardi B posted six nonsensical videos over the course of two weeks, one of which was a repost of another person's video, taken from a different social media platform. It didn't matter that she then posted two more videos a month later, and a final two nine months later. They didn't want, or consider the importance of, engagement with the platform. They just wanted to say she was there.

It was an issue for the American staffers tasked with carrying out those commands from Beijing. Staff felt their Chinese counterparts were trying to fit a square peg into a round hole, utilising the same playbook that had brought them success in China but wouldn't and couldn't work in the West. Their local knowledge was overlooked, employees felt, by people who outranked them and could get the ear of the key decision makers by dint of their proximity in the central Beijing office. It was accentuated by a difference in organisational philosophy.

In the West, one former employee said, you hire people based on their experience, their skill set, and the proven evidence they can do the job you're asking them to do. The employee's experience with the Chinese side of the business was that bosses took a different approach altogether: 'throw a warm body at it and some funding and, you know, they'll figure it out.' They made up a hypothetical example that they stressed wasn't too far from the truth of the chaotic early days of ByteDance's global expansion: the company could have a 25-year-old sat in Beijing in charge of global user acquisition, who had control of a multi-million dollar budget, who had no experience of user acquisition at all. (Employees also trade war stories of a woman put in charge of global marketing because she had managed to land Douyin a tie-in with a Chinese TV talent show that superpowered growth in China. She was tasked with doing the same thing everywhere else in the world, with diminishing returns.) It's easy to see, given that hypothetical example that wasn't too far wide of the mark, how it's possible to spend six figures on an uninterested rapper who puts minimal effort into a handful of videos then deserts the platform forever more.

But those experiences stung – and in the early days, the manufactured flops like Cardi B outnumbered the organic successes like Schwarzenegger. That, coupled with the resentment that the scrappy, small offices in the United States were being leant on and dictated to by ByteDance central office in Beijing, meant that the formative few years of TikTok in the United States weren't always happy ones. Around the same time as Cardi B half-heartedly returned to the app – for a sponsored competition she was contractually obliged to plug to win VIP tickets to two music festivals, a trip to Disneyland, a smartphone, some clothes and TikTok branded goodies – ByteDance conducted an employee satisfaction survey.

The findings were sobering. Pretty much every employee reporting to a boss in Beijing reported low satisfaction levels.

Since then, things have changed. As we'll learn, political necessity, plus an acknowledgement that it's not possible for people based in Beijing to possibly know the cultural tastes of middle America better than those closer to the audience, means that employee satisfaction has improved in TikTok's satellite offices – largely. There are still some issues. ByteDance began to realise it couldn't simply repeat the exact same success, step for step, with TikTok in the West.

23
CENSORSHIP:
AN EAST-WEST DIVIDE

ByteDance knows that it cannot allow the same things to be shown in China and the West.

Internal documents given to moderators working on TikTok by ByteDance outline the kind of things that are and aren't allowed on the platform. Until May 2019, when the policy changed, TikTok would not recommend videos that included imagery of a political figure, unless they were 'in a private setting or acting as a private individual.' Not recommending the videos would throttle their reach, meaning people would have to proactively search for a user's content rather than coming across it on the For You page, the main way that people interact with TikTok. Likewise, any content depicting politically sensitive events in a number of countries, including Northern Irish independence, the 'indipendence' [sic] of Taiwan and Tibet, the Tiananmen Square incident, or the 2014 Ukrainian revolution was given the status of 'VTS', or visible to self. That meant that while the user didn't realise it, and was able to view their own videos on the subject on TikTok, no one else could.

After September 2019, following a significant outcry that Chinese state censorship was bleeding through to a global platform, that changed from a worldwide prohibition on TikTok to guidance for moderators to assess specific enforcement of the rules based on local sensitivities. It was a 'blunt approach,' TikTok admitted to The *Guardian*, and an indication of the growing pains seen by the platform as it aimed to shift from operating in a state-controlled country to being a borderless multinational organisation. A spokesperson explained: 'As TikTok began to take off globally [in 2018], we recognised that this was not the correct approach, and began working to empower local teams that have a nuanced understanding of each market.'

That works, up to a point. A 17-year-old student at a New Jersey high school, Feroza Aziz, who tried to explain the imprisonment of Uyghur Muslims inside concentration camps within China, found her profile repeatedly blocked and deleted. Aziz found her videos didn't gain much traction on the platform, either because viewers were not interested in a history lesson or because TikTok's algorithm had artificially suppressed them. (She had a hunch which it was.) So she decided on subterfuge to get across her message. Sitting in front of the camera with a powder blue hair scrunchy wrapped around her wrist and an eyelash crimper in her hand, she began offering appearance tips – and commentary on a geopolitical issue that would otherwise have fallen foul of the app's moderation policies.

Aziz was smart. She realised that the way content moderators parse videos was by watching small snippets of suspect videos. According to insiders who work in TikTok's moderation teams in Europe, every employee overseeing the videos posted onto the app is expected to check through around 1,000 videos in an eight-hour shift. When I asked Cormac Keenan, TikTok's global head of trust and safety, whether he could accurately monitor 1,000 videos a day, he didn't respond directly to the question. Given breaks and flagging attention spans, moderators have less than half a minute to make a decision on whether any video falls foul of TikTok's stringent rules. Borderline content may take several minutes to consider, meaning they will probably skip over other videos quickly. They aren't encouraged to watch the whole video, either: they are told that unless they think a video merits a closer look they should skip through individual frames and don't need to listen to the sound.

If a moderator came across Aziz's video, they would probably think it was just a girl curling her eyelashes. In the unlikely event they bothered to listen to the first few seconds, they would also not find anything amiss. 'Hi guys, I'm going to teach you guys how to get long lashes,' Aziz begins, clamping the curler around her eyelashes. 'The first thing you need to do is grab your lash curler, curl your lashes obviously, then you can put them down.' Only after eight seconds does Aziz encourage her viewers to search 'what's happening in China, how they're getting concentration camps and throwing innocent Muslims in there.'

It was only after the video blew up on TikTok and on Twitter, where it was reposted and viewed five million times, that the content moderators realised what had happened. TikTok suspended Aziz's profile. It said that was because on another account she had previously posted a video about Osama Bin Laden that violated its content policies regarding 'terrorist imagery.' TikTok later reinstated her main account, but with her content deleted. Aziz said: 'Do I believe they took it away because of an unrelated satirical video that was deleted on a previous deleted account of mine? Right after I finished posting a three-part video about the Uyghurs? No.'

TikTok's Chinese-centric sensitivities aren't the only things causing headaches for the app. Policies that aim to straddle the world can also be a problem. Videos about sexual orientation and gender identity are given their own sections in the content moderation policy. There, content moderators are advised to append a 'risk tag' to each video: an indicator that the video contains questionable content for some more conservative countries in which the app operates. In those countries, content tagged as a risk won't be displayed in the For You feed. TikTok said that was for its users' safety. Its overly censorious approaches to videos can be bizarre: Dr Carolina Are, who has researched why some of the world's most-used apps censor women, was herself the victim of repeated bans on TikTok, triggered by sensitive viewers deciding they didn't like her posting videos of her fully clothed pole dancing. The irony wasn't lost on many.

Fat people and those with unusual bodies have also been discriminated against. Open up any social media app and you're confronted with an array of people preening and presenting themselves in perfectly posed selfies. Part of that is with the help of gadgetry and gizmos: a ring light, a halo of warm luminescence that can be bought and attached to a smartphone to give the perfect lighting for your cheekbones and chin, can help smooth the ravages of real life. After-photo touch-ups courtesy of a range of apps that pinch and tuck imperfections have changed what it's like to be a human being. But the documentation given to TikTok moderators makes explicit what social media's natural selection cycle suggests: if you're fat, you aren't making it.

When it's put down in black and white type, the rules around what's allowed and what isn't on TikTok seem stark. If you're unlucky enough to be in possession of an 'Abnormal body shape, chubby, have obvious beer belly, obese, or too thin (not limited to: dwarf, acromegaly),' then your video's reach will be curtailed. Have 'Ugly facial looks (not limited to: disformatted face, fangs, lack of front teeth, senior people with too many wrinkles, obvious facial scars) or facial deformities (not limited to: eye disorders, crooked mouth disease and other disabilities)'? You're out of luck.

The motivation is the same as that which ends up with good-looking people presenting TV programmes – we are attracted to attractive people. 'If the character's appearance or the shooting environment is not good, the video will be much less attractive, not worthing [sic] to be recommended to new users.'

If you're poor, and your walls aren't pristine, you're also out of luck. If you have a 'shabby and dilapidated' shooting environment, your video isn't likely to be promoted – because it's 'not that suitable for new users,' to whom TikTok wants to portray the perfect image. Subpar shooting environments include, but aren't limited to, videos being shot in 'slums, rural fields, [and] dilapidated housing.' The message is clear: if you want to go viral, be rich – or at the very least, clean up.

Until September 2019, German-based moderators were told that people who had facial disfigurements, autism, Down Syndrome or 'some facial problems such as birthmark, slight squint and etc' should have their videos' reach limited. The justification was a simple one: such disfigurements could make them 'highly vulnerable to cyberbullying.' UK disability equality charity Scope called the decision 'bizarre.'

It's an issue TikTok realised it should correct. In March 2020, as part of a fightback against an increasingly hostile political backdrop in the US, the app announced that it would be forming an independent committee 'to provide unvarnished views on and advice around TikTok's policies and practices.' David Ryan Polgar, a tech ethicist, had been contacted by TikTok in December 2019 and asked if he would fly to London to talk to executives about how to improve content moderation. He was paid for the trip, and his expenses and flights covered. It's something he's done for countless companies. 'It's something I'm quite direct about,' says Polgar: 'I've been saying for years I think [tech companies] are in over their head in the sense that they've really been pushed with a lot of power they're not necessarily well-equipped to handle.'

He said that tech firms were in an odd position: 'You have private companies now acting in the capacity that traditionally resides in a governmental oversight.... I think they realise which way the wind is blowing, and they want to be more forward about it.' His role – and that of his companions on the board – is to challenge TikTok on some of the issues they were likely to face, to learn about the struggles TikTok could face as a platform, and to come up with possible solutions. The council has already discussed issues around the different perception of videos depending on whether you're a young creator or an older consumer. What may be considered a playful, joyous and innocent dance by a 15-year-old girl can be thought of as something altogether more sexual by older audiences. How do you handle such disparate views of the same video? Do you limit the reach of the video in order to head off the potential harm of someone viewing it maliciously, or is that unfair to the person who produced it innocently? 'If you're just thinking internally you're going to think about it from one perspective, whereas I think you have to think not just about how this person is presenting the information but also how it's received, and how you change the dynamics,' says Polgar, who admits that the policy is a work in progress.

Content moderation is difficult for TikTok, in large part because it is complicated. TikTok is a company steeped in Chinese culture and norms trying to expand its viewpoint to take in a panoply of different opinions. An American consumer has a wildly different viewpoint on what is acceptable to a Chinese one. And an Indian user is likely to be much more sensitive in certain areas than others. That's a challenge for a company that still has large elements of its operations centralised within one of the most repressive, insular and censorious countries in the world outside North Korea.

Until recently, community moderators working on deciding what is and what isn't acceptable in massive world regions such as Latin America did so from crowded shared desks in ByteDance's offices in Beijing. While they were often native speakers from the countries they were moderating, they had moved to China, and operated within a Chinese culture. However, the last TikTok moderator left the Chinese capital in summer 2020, according to the company. In June 2021, Cormac Keenan told me that all 10,000 of TikTok's global content moderators were based outside China. He said: 'We've got a global strategy now where we're building locations for our moderation efforts around the world.'

The troubles over moderation are yet another instance where a clash of cultures causes problems, where Zhang's idyllic dream of becoming as borderless as Google bumps up against reality. One former employee believes ByteDance's missteps on content and culture have been the result of its speedy success. 'I wouldn't want to try and run a Chinese company in China from over here, if I've never really been there and learned a lot about it,' they said.

'They really did hinder a lot of stuff, especially in the US. But the product is so good.'

CREATOR FOCUS
SPARKS AND TARTS

Name: Danny Harris
Username: @sparksandtarts
Following: 14
Followers: 68K
Likes: 501.5K
Speciality: Dancing on building sites, wearing high-vis jackets

Danny Harris didn't expect to become a TikTok star when he started working at a building site in Covent Garden in the centre of London, but then he hadn't heard of the app back then. It took a fellow labourer coming into the site's office one day in late 2019 during a downtime break and showing them a handful of videos they'd liked on the app for them to get the bug. The choreographed, carefully tuned dancing they saw enthralled them – and better yet, they thought they could give it a go themselves.

At first it was a joke – a bit of building site bravado from one of the workers. But as anyone who's ever eavesdropped on a conversation between blue-collar workers knows, once you've made a daring claim, you have to back it up. The others laughed at the joke, then they cajoled him into doing it. 'It took on its own head of steam,' says Harris, 35. Suddenly a small troupe of workers wearing hard hats and high-visibility jackets and vests downed tools and picked up a set of dance steps they had to follow to the letter.

The first video, which saw Harris and four colleagues performing a rudimentary but sassy sashay to a song from the musical Pitch Perfect, was seen a million times in the first month. Harris started being recognised at the bakery down the road from the building site when grabbing his lunch.

A combination of personal pride, and momentum on social media, coaxed some of the more sceptical colleagues in front of the camera. Suddenly there were a dozen or so participants who would gather during breaks over flasks and mugs of builder's tea to brainstorm the next viral video hit. Mobile phone messages ping-ponged between the groups linking out to other videos they could perform their own take on. The most committed even choreographed dance moves with their kids at home at weekends and sent around rough videos blocking out movements, encouraging their colleagues to memorise the steps. They had become influencers: they were called Sparks and Tarts – a combination of their labourer background, and a cheeky wink to their exuberant videos.

If it's all a bit unusual for a group of grown men who in the stereotype are more likely to wolf whistle at passing women than to prance about for the entertainment of millions online, that's the point. 'We try and go for the silliest and most camp we can,' explains Harris. 'It's breaking a few stereotypes of what people expect people in uniform to be like. There's a bit of a stigma that none of us can even drag our knuckles across the floor.' By acting the fool, and performing with a well-arched eyebrow, as well as a well-arched back as they strike a pose, they're striking a blow against the norm.

The success hasn't gone to their heads yet – the first brand deal was a surprise. A drinks company sent them some merchandise, and a high-visibility clothing firm got in touch asking if they'd like to wear their products in their videos. 'When you realise how many people are viewing your video, it really sinks in,' says Harris. 'It really resonates in your head.'

PART V

CREATIVITY

24
CHANGING WHAT
MUSIC MEANS

TikTok has seeped into culture into manifest ways, but probably its greatest impact has been on music. As vinyl records gave way to tapes, and tapes to CDs – before all were brushed aside by the dominance of digital music downloading and streaming – the music industry struggled to make money. Without the impetus to go out and buy a physical album or single anymore, mainstream music shows have disappeared from TV guides. MTV transformed from a channel airing music videos to one that shows reality TV shows on an endless, hellish loop.

Talent had to tour the world, dragging themselves from one identikit arena to another in order to scrape a living. Until TikTok, there was no suitable short-form visual medium where they could promote their new releases, so they relied on their core audience, struggling to make it to new listeners.

TikTok has revitalised the flagging music industry by driving listeners who hear a small section of a song on TikTok videos to music streaming platforms like Spotify or YouTube, where someone listening to the song returns a small sliver of revenue to the artist – and more importantly, something that translates into a music chart position. One music industry executive said that TikTok was the new radio. TikTok's UK managing director reckons official music charts should take into account TikTok views when calculating who should be top of the pops. So too does Paul Hourican, TikTok's head of music operations. 'TikTok drives off-platform consumption of songs,' he says. 'Success on TikTok is phenomenal at driving consumption of your music.'

As a long-time music industry insider, Hourican is well placed to comment. He had spent a decade at MTV in the early 2000s before moving to YouTube as its head of music curation, ending up in New York as YouTube's head of international artist marketing. Like many expats in a foreign land, he reached a point where he and his family had to decide where they wanted to spend the rest of their lives and, in 2019, he flew back to the UK to look for a new job.

On 8 October 2019, he had a job interview at TikTok – but beforehand he was working the room at an event held at the O2 London by the industry magazine *Music Week*. Its second annual tech summit was taking place, with the industry's movers and shakers meeting to look at how technology can change music – and music could interact with tech.

Hourican had seen the impact of Musical.ly and TikTok on the music industry. At the conference he couldn't escape the company. 'Every conversation at the *Music Week* tech conference turned into a conversation about TikTok,' he recalls. When the time came for his job interview, he scurried off to a corner of the O2. His mind was made up. 'I'm in,' he said. 'This is something I wanted to do. That's how I decided to join.'

The reason was simple. Hourican, who since November 2019 has headed TikTok's music operations in the UK, had a hunch about the app's success. The chatter around the conference's side-lines helped firm that up. TikTok has 'basically reinvented the way people want to communicate with one another,' he says. 'It's the perfect creative medium to bind things together.' And it's borne out in the data. Four in five TikTok users say they visit the app to discover new music, according to internal polling data commissioned by the company.

Hourican says that users on TikTok hear a small snippet of a song in the most attractive way possible – alongside engaging video content – and want to hear more. That drives them to seek out the longer track itself, and to find out more about the artist. It's for that reason that TikTok sees itself as a net benefit to the music industry, rather than a competitor. 'It's very much additive, and not cannibalistic,' he says.

25
DOJA CAT'S
STORY

Nicki Minaj had been producing music for 16 years until the moment came. The Trinidadian-born, New York-raised singer had contributed to plenty of earworms since she first performed on a music track professionally in 2004, but had never had a number one hit on the Billboard Hot 100, America's pop music charts. Amalaratna Zandile Dlamini, better known professionally as Doja Cat, a name she came up with after combining her love of cats and her favourite strain of marijuana, had to wait nearly seven years for her first hit. When it came on 11 May 2020, the plaudits were huge. *Say So*, the pair's song, raced up the charts to the very top. And the reason was simple. TikTok.

The small section of Doja Cat's *Say So* put on TikTok by her label has been used in more than 13 million videos, including at least five in the course of one week before Christmas by Charli D'Amelio, TikTok's biggest star. D'Amelio repeatedly posted videos of her performing a choreographed dance to the song, which combined were liked by her fans 20 million times. The videos propelled the song into the public consciousness. It was mission accomplished for Jacob Pace, the 22-year-old who had masterminded the rise.

Pace got involved in the music industry at the age of 14, setting up a YouTube channel that provided him an outlet to promote his own music. He set up a record label shortly after, then started doing social media for a record label and a PR firm. He flew out from El Paso, Texas to Los Angeles when he was 16, hired by a record label to run their artists and repertoire (A&R) business development and marketing work. At 18 he came across a profile on Musical.ly called Flighthouse that was proving popular. Pace noticed that it was one of the only large accounts on Musical.ly. It compiled music, and he recognised that it was different. Many of the other pages on Musical.ly belonged to individual influencers, who struggled to cut through the noise. But Flighthouse was a brand. The company Pace worked for acquired it, and gave it to Pace to run. 'When TikTok came to be a thing, it worked out well for us,' he says, sounding more mature than his young years. He grew the Flighthouse account to become the 15th biggest on TikTok, and set up a marketing agency around the Flighthouse brand. One of the artists the agency helped gain ground on TikTok was Doja Cat.

'It's been a great way for audiences to discover and be a part of music,' says Pace. The organisation does 20 or 30 music placements a month, including Doja Cat's tracks.

A music label sends Pace and Flighthouse a record. The company listens to the track and figures out the most viral element that could work on TikTok as a clip against which users can record their videos. It then conceive a trend that will be associated with the video – probably a dance, a reaction or a skit – and send it back to the label. Once approved by the record label, Flighthouse sends the trend to its network of influencers to roll out on the app, starting with 10 or 20 at first. 'We'll give them the song, see what sticks, and if something doesn't stick, we'll iterate the trend idea,' says Pace. 'Our goal is to see there's viral momentum there.' The yardstick by which the campaigns are measured is the number of videos created.

The scheme is real-world A/B testing, where you see whether something thrives or dies – and change plans accordingly. A return of 100 organically made videos by ordinary users who have seen the 10 influencer-seeded videos on TikTok isn't a success, and is a sign that Flighthouse needs to go back to the drawing board. But if the same 10 influencer-led, and Flighthouse-designed videos give birth to 50,000 videos from rank and file users, it's a success. 'That's a sign for us to be putting in more money,' says Pace. Sources close to the campaigns Flighthouse runs say that music labels have to fork out a minimum of $50,000 for a basic campaign.

It's a similar story elsewhere in the world: music labels, recognising the power of TikTok to propel their artists up the charts, are starting to deal with companies that can help them reach that goal. JP Saxe's song *If the World Was Ending*, featuring Julia Michaels, is a laidback, morose piano song about one man's love for a woman. Released in October 2019, the song was pushed onto TikTok, where a hashtag (#IfTheWorldWasEnding) was created and a handful of the 6,000 influencers London-based content marketing agency Fanbytes work with were contacted and asked to use the song. The planned posts were staggered out so it seemed organic, and the result was success. Videos that used the hashtag were seen 28 million times; more than 700,000 videos were created not just by the influencers approached, but everyday users. Campaigns for Fanbytes start at £5,000 and scale up to around £30,000 for more significant packages. The song jumped 25 places in a week on the Official UK Singles Chart to spot number 16 – all thanks to TikTok.

But if you want an example of a life changed thanks to TikTok, you need look no further than Monero Lamar Hill, the 22-year-old better known the world over as Lil Nas X. Hill grew up in Georgia, attending Lithia Springs High School until he graduated in 2017. In his early years in high school, he was an active participant on all sorts of social media platforms, including Vine. After Lithia Springs, he decided to go to college, to study computer science – an extension of the hours of time the nerdy child spent on his computer in some of the darkest corners of the internet, developing odd memes that only the most internet-literate browsers would recognise. Hill did well at college, but dropped out after a year on his course. 'I didn't want to do school anymore,' he told *Teen Vogue*. Within months of leaving, he had released his first album, which he called *Naserati*, on Soundcloud, a website overflowing with songs posted by artists looking for their big break online.

The album didn't get much attention, and his parents became worried. With six children, including one son who had been imprisoned, they were worried college drop-out Monero, whose attempt to make it as a musician was faltering in fits and starts, could soon go down the same path. He spent too much time on his phone, they said, and not enough time thinking about the future if he didn't make it. He moved in with his sister, who had also put up another sister. The move gave Hill the freedom to tinker, but he still wasn't making progress. Then his sister began to find the living arrangement, two other siblings and her own children crammed under the same roof, untenable. She asked Hill to find his own place. He had reached the Old Town Road, and was running away – riding until he couldn't anymore.

Now out on his own, Hill threw himself into making more music. He spent hours scrolling through sample beats on websites that sell music with which to make backing tracks for songs. On one, he found a beat by a 19-year-old called Kiowa Roukema. Roukema had built a reputation on BeatStars, where he went by the name YoungKio, for posting beats he made in music production software FruityLoops. Roukema was given the software by a friend at the age of 16. He had previously earned a little cash making backgrounds for YouTubers.

At first, Roukema uploaded the beats he produced – sometimes sampling a single instrument from a more popular track – onto YouTube and sold them for a $20 lease. Every odd song he searched for to sample helped hone YouTube's algorithm – the black box computer code that serves a user videos it believes they'll like – until one day a song by the band Nine Inch Nails appeared in Roukema's recommended videos list.

Roukema had never heard of the rock band, and enjoyed the banjos playing in the track. He immediately thought the instrument could be sampled and turned into the backing beat for various songs. He added drums underneath the banjo and posted the sample onto BeatStars as a 'future type beat.' At that point, Hill came across the beat and downloaded it, spending around $30. He saw it as a representation of 'a sad cowboy going through some shit,' and saw similarities in his life. In exchange, Roukema would get a 50% share of all the profits of any songs made using the beat. The song that Hill – also known as Lil Nas X – made using the beat was *Old Town Road*.

Lil Nas X uploaded it to Soundcloud in December 2018, and encountered the same problems he had with *Naserati*. It didn't really gain much traction on the site, but did on TikTok, where it was picked up and transformed into a challenge called the Yeehaw challenge, where people transform out of their ordinary clothes and into cowboy boots to the backing of the song. *Old Town Road* went viral on TikTok, and then the world. Lil Nas X, who had struggled to get himself out of a fug just a few months earlier, was on top of the world.

The song was remixed with country star Billy Ray Cyrus, and went top of the Billboard Hot 100 charts – the longest such run in history. 'I am so thankful this blessing has been placed upon me,' Lil Nas X posted on Instagram, punctuated by various emojis. 'This song has changed my life and the way I see the world around me in less than a year.' Other musicians are seeing the benefits of TikTok to propel them to stardom – but aren't seeing commensurate returns.

26
TIKTOK
MASH-UP

TikTok isn't just giving new artists an opportunity to make a living. It's also changing what music means.

And some artists aren't just combining music and video together: they're combining pre-existing music in a way that works intrinsically for TikTok.

Jacob Feldman was in his teens when Vine became popular. The Los Angelino teen first downloaded the app in 2014, and enjoyed its unparalleled creativity. He particularly liked the subsection of the site devoted to music. He would spend hours on his computer programming music tracks he thought would be of interest.

Feldman began to see a potential crossover for his two passions. He set up an account on the app under the name Plot Twist, and set himself a challenge: uploading a single track every day that would seamlessly transition from one song to another. The name was a straightforward way of explaining Feldman's conceit. You could start listening to one song, then at the skip of a single beat it'd move to another song. It was unexpected and interesting. Plot Twist gained popularity. By the time Vine shut down, Feldman's account on the app had 600,000 followers. Songs he had shunted together digitally to create something new were used in videos seen more than 500 million times.

Just before Vine shut down, and while Feldman was starting his studies at Berkeley School of Music in Boston, he found a better fit for his musical talent. An app called Musical.ly was starting to rise up the app store rankings, and it was a good fit for Feldman's skills. So he began cross-posting his content to both platforms: Musical.ly and Vine. He also had a YouTube account where he posted full versions of the songs he mashed up, but found that copyright issues made it not worth his time trying to upload too often.

One of Feldman's favourite songs to use for his Plot Twist account was Soulja Boy's 2007 cult classic song *Crank That*. The track itself isn't enormously inventive: it's repetitive, and the lyrics go nowhere. But it's an earworm, and best of all, its backing beat makes it easy to switch into and out of.

Feldman's process for mashing up songs was semi-industrialised. He had a vast back catalogue of tracks on his computer, sorted by beats per minute and key, and matched up songs that were in the same key and had equal rhythm. 'I actually mixed the Soulja Boy with other songs too that were popular, like *Drag Me Down* by One Direction,' says Feldman. 'Since I was making it every day, I had to think of a new one every single day, and I was combining anything I could think of.'

His music had moderate success on Musical.ly, but it wasn't until his account was automatically transferred over to TikTok after the merger, that he really began to make a name for himself. Feldman creates some of the most commonly used tracks on TikTok, combining any number of popular songs together to create a new one. Some of them have even more views than bona fide number one hits made popular on TikTok like *Old Town Road*. Yet the sum total of all Feldman's income streams from music amounts to no more than $100 a month because he doesn't own the copyright to any of the songs he fuses.

Many people would argue that's fair. Pop stars and musicians put days and weeks of their lives into creating new songs, and take vast financial risks in doing so. Feldman just takes songs he already knows are popular, splices them together, and uploads them under his name. Yet it still takes time and effort – Feldman estimates he spends two hours on each mashup. He's responsible for many of the trends that go mega viral on the platform. He just doesn't get any recognition. Others are getting that recognition, long after they first found fame as musicians.

27
ONE HIT
WONDERS

Matthew Wilder is the dictionary definition of a one-hit wonder. He spent the late 1970s providing backing vocals for a number of more successful singers, before managing to climb up near the top of the charts in 1983 with *Break My Stride*, an upbeat, perky song about how nothing's going to break his stride, and nobody's going to slow him down. It was written as a howl of anguish at his former record label, Arista, which signed Wilder to a contract then did little to progress his career. He appeared on music TV shows and was set up for future success – until second single syndrome hit. Wilder's follow-up to *Break My Stride*, *The Kid's American*, did nowhere near as well. The second album he released flopped. And for the best part of 25 years, Wilder was nothing more than a cult classic and an answer to a relatively uninteresting pub quiz question.

But the ethos of the song, and the jaunty music behind it, gained it a second wind. In 2020, *Break My Stride* had a resurgence as TikTok users rediscovered the song and began using it in their videos. At first they did so through a meme of texting the lyrics, line by line, to their older relatives and waiting to see if the penny dropped. Others then just started dancing along to the chorus. Wilder's brother first noticed *Break My Stride* was surging in popularity thanks to a Google alert he had set up to advise him to any coverage of his brother's career. Around the same time, his record label, Sony, sent Feldman a note to ask if he had noticed a bunch of kids born years after his song was big were starting to use it on this strange app called TikTok.

It was all a surprise to the 68-year-old. He gamely agreed to set up his own TikTok account and record a video, where he eerily appears through the mists of a malfunctioning green screen, wrapped up in an off-white duvet, to act out the lyrics to the song in front of a text message background – an homage to his resurgence in popularity. For the first time in years, Wilder ended up in the music charts once more off the back of his TikTok success. 'The fact that all these things have such a long life and are able to come back and be appreciated again and again, speaks to the depths of what we were capable of doing,' he told the BBC. 'I'm thrilled. To go beyond that would be overstating or repeating myself, but I'm thrilled.'

He's not the only one. Just as Mariah Carey was experiencing a second wind thanks to Jacob Feldman using her Christmas classic *All I Want for Christmas is You* in a Plot Twist track, another remarkable resurgence was occurring on German-speaking TikTok, overlooked by many. At Christmas, German-speaking families like nothing more than coming together as a group and baking biscuits and cakes to celebrate the holidays. The trend of *Weihnachtsbäckerei* (Christmas baking) extended to TikTok, too, with the hashtag #Weihnachtsbäckerei trending on German-language TikTok since 10 December. And a good number of those videos of Christmas biscuits being carefully rolled, cut and iced were soundtracked by a single song performed by a German cult hero who's now a 72-year-old man happily living out his retirement.

Rolf Zuckowski became a hero in Germany and German-speaking countries in 1987 when he recorded a child-friendly ditty detailing the chaos that ensues when you start splashing around sugar, flour and butter in the days before Christmas. The song's name was *In der Weihnachtsbäckerei* ('In the Christmas bakery'). It was a song that Zuckowski had come up with to celebrate his own family's Christmas in 1986, and when he officially released it a year later it joined the pantheon of Christmas music, slapped onto every family's Christmas music cassettes and CDs. But it was always a bit kitsch: children loved it in their formative years, then outgrew it. Until it joined TikTok, and became the soundtrack to many people's 2019 Christmas celebrations. 'For me it is like a gift from heaven,' Zuckowski told me when I caught up with him a week before Christmas that year. He was grateful for TikTok: 'Social media now plays an important part in spreading the message to all generations, every year again.'

28
THE CONVENTION
CENTRE, 2020

You can spot them by the brightness of their clothing, and the fact that they are standing stock still in the middle of a busy convention centre corridor. It is February 2020 and I am back at VidCon London.

There in front of the chi-chi bakery selling overpriced sandwiches are the Neffati Brothers. To pass them on the street, Jamil and Jamel Neffati wouldn't stand out: they are heavily tattooed, necks and forearms stained deeply with blotches of ink, with strong, broad noses and a cheeky smile. Their dangling earrings and dyed hair styled into matching gentle quiffs don't distinguish them from anyone in 2020. In another world they could be builders in their native Poland, or the altogether non-stagey home town they have adopted in Blackburn, England. But when you put them in the middle of VidCon and dress them up in matching bright orange t-shirts, among some of the 13.2 million people who watch their every move on TikTok, they are bound to grab attention. Especially when they're standing in formation as if they're part of the Red Arrows, heads bowed, hands crossed in front of their waist, and a man with a small camera attached to a pole is scuttling away in the opposite direction away from them.

We are all about to be treated to a TikTok being filmed in the wild.

I am walking through the conference centre with Zoe Glatt and YouTuber Simon Clark, who will later produce educational content around his particular area of expertise – climate science – when we spot the odd grouping. We linger for a while, and Clark breaks out his camera, for which he is filming a vlog for his YouTube channel.

We wait for a while. The cameraman scampers away, setting up what looks like a long zoom in to the dancing troupe – likely sped up before returning back to normal speed to make a dramatic start to the video. But he goes further than most people expect: about two-thirds of the way along the 600-metre venue. And the need to steady the camera, especially given any bounce or blur will be accentuated by the speeding up of the footage, means his hare-like dash away from the Neffati Brothers becomes a cautious, tortoise-like tip-toe back to them. It's something the earliest film-makers, from Charlie Chaplin on, recognised as a problem. Small wobbles made in slow motion, when sped up, become jolts resembling a drive up a mountainside.

Eventually, he gets there, then stops. There is a second or two's pause, before the twins leap into action. They look over their shoulders, one by one, the backing dancers doing the same.

That is it. The cameraman holds the shot for a second. They hold their pose. Then they wander off, joining another set of twins for another collaborative video.

The incident is... underwhelming, to say the least, but it is emblematic of the new norm in social media. Just as it's taken several years to not look twice at an unbearably attractive young thing brandishing a Canon EOS 5D atop a JOBY GuerillaPod at arm's length, energetically gesticulating at the camera for their YouTube channel, we are still in the early stages of the rise of TikTok, and the sight of people spontaneously meeting to perform intricately choreographed dances is still unusual. You see it on social media: videos posted from afar poke fun at the careful planning that goes into creating TikToks. The app's own social media accounts are even guilty of it, sharing videos of people performing frantic dances to perched-up phones without the benefit of the background music that contextualises them.

TikTok is taking over VidCon. The video sharing conference has long been supported by YouTube, which has seen the younger, shorter-form upstart as competition. This time, TikTok appears at more panels – but they are almost all sponsored by the company itself. It is paying to play. The exhibition hall, where online video creators hawk their own merchandise to exhausted pre-teens, is presented by TikTok.

The hottest ticket at VidCon London 2020 is the TikTok party, held at a basement cellar bar in Shoreditch. Guests need a luminescent paper wristband – and the chatter at the exclusive creator lounges is how to snag one.

It is clear that the sands are shifting in the online video world, and what was once firmly within YouTube's control is suddenly up for grabs. What a difference a year has made. And what a difference another year would make: in June 2021, TikTok supplanted YouTube as VidCon's official sponsor – a sign of the rapid change in the online video market.

CREATOR FOCUS
HANK GREEN

Name: Hank Green
Username: @hankgreen1
Following: 837
Followers: 7.1 million
Likes: 503.1 million
Speciality: Explaining the world

TikTok isn't Hank Green's first rodeo. The 42-year-old, who lives in Missoula, Montana, is one of the digital world's most recognisable names. Green was a blogger and writer for a number of websites that were chock-full of trivia, educating people about the world in which they live.

But it was in 2007 when he turned to YouTube with his brother, John – now a famous author – to create the Vlogbrothers channel. The Green brothers became some of YouTube's earliest celebrities, followed by a flock of slightly geeky, entirely wholesome adherents called the Nerdfighters. They set up podcasts, sold socks, and fundraise for charity every year. In 2010, the brothers also launched Vidcon, an online video convention that brought together the scattered solar system of online video stars together, which Hank continues to oversee even after its purchase by Viacom.

Green is a bona fide internet celebrity – but success on TikTok didn't come easy. 'I started on TikTok a couple of times,' he says, firstly in 2019. 'I posted a video, and it didn't do well, so a year later I posted a video... and it didn't do well.' Green reckons he had to wait until TikTok was ready for him, and he was ready for TikTok, in large part through the creator base maturing from its relatively young early core. 'I had to wait for it to get to a certain level of maturity before it would have me,' he says. 'It felt initially like this was definitely not a place for someone who was born in the 1980s.'

Still, Green persisted. The main thing that drew him back to the platform was him indirectly becoming the focus of a meme on TikTok. Throughout the spring of 2020, the theme music for CrashCourse, an educational YouTube series Green and his brother established, had been repurposed as part of a meme where people would stand in front of a profound – or profoundly silly – tweet using TikTok's green screen technology.

So on May 22 2020, Green posted another TikTok. Using the same audio, he transposed himself in front of a tweet reading: 'Ok, can someone explain to me the TikTok meme where people green screen themselves in front of a screenshot of a tweet and the CrashCourse theme plays?'. The video was seen three million times.

'The people who suggested I join TikTok were all very exited for me,' he says. 'From there, it was kind of a process of figuring out what my role was, what would succeed, and what people would like.' Handily, Green had been doing that job for nearly 15 years by then. He ended up taking on a similar role to that on YouTube: someone who explains the world. But he also acknowledged that in his forties, he would have to adopt a patrician position to his followers, many of whom were young enough to be his children.

Green also recognised that TikTok, and its algorithm, was something different to what had gone before. 'It takes something that has proved popular and interesting, and that people like, and just shoots that out everywhere to hit a lot of feeds,' he says. That's how you end up with TikToks that you've never really seen and aren't big cultural phenomena, but have 100 million views a day.

He adopted an elder statesman role, educating his younger audience about subjects from science to history – and everything in between.

And given his long history with online video platforms, Green sees some key similarities and differences between the shortform app and others that have gone before it. 'The best thing about TikTok is that that allows for the discovery of new talent,' he says. 'And the worst thing is that it prevents that it does not show clear paths for that new talent to find any kind of economic sustainability or value outside of attention.'

Green doesn't know whether that's necessarily a problem for TikTok: he thinks that enough people might want to have the first flourish of fame to continue to feed the maw of content needed to populate the app, and will replace those who end up frustrated that they can't make a living out of it and leave.

That, he reckons, could be what puts paid to the app – along with the way in which TikTok rides and creates the zeitgeist. 'It's not a moat,' he explains, that can prevent any newcomers from usurping the app. 'Things like that are inherently fragile, because they have to be cool, and to be cool, you have to be new.' TikTok is cool right now, 'but nothing stays cool forever. And nothing even stays cool for long.'

That said, Green managed to win over the kids on TikTok while in his forties. He laughs at that. 'But I'm not cool,' he says. 'That's my trick. My secret.'

CREATOR FOCUS
GRANDAD JOE

Name: Joe Allington
Username: @grandadjoe1933
Following: 36
Followers: 4.3M
Likes: 103.2M
Speciality: Stealing and eating biscuits without his family knowing; giving life advice to youngsters

Joe Allington enjoyed his retirement from a job in the road haulage industry. He would sit on a bench in a local park in the Midlands with his wife, whiling away the time. After his wife died in 2009, he lived alone for a few years, but his daughter Wendy eventually convinced him to move in with her and the kids in mid-2015.

Life among his children and grandchildren opened Allington's eyes to the odd quirks of younger generations. He was baffled by the amount of time his grandchildren in particular spent on their smartphones chatting to friends. His youngest grandchild, Brooke, Wendy's daughter, confused him when she started dancing in front of her camera. She was 16 at the time, and had just discovered TikTok.

Brooke slowly started pestering her grandfather to try and join him in mouthing along to the pop songs she performed to. Allington wasn't willing at first. Then his daughter joined in the cajoling, and he started doing small bits of acting for videos. He got a taste for it. 'It's taken off from there,' he explains over a crackling phone line set up by his daughter, because he couldn't figure out how to make it work. 'I quite enjoy being made up, dressed up and made a fool of.'

Aged 88, he's known as Grandad Joe on the app and is followed by 4.3 million people on TikTok. His videos have been liked 103 million times. His daughter had to tell him when he crossed a million followers; he couldn't quite believe it, and had to grab his own iPhone to check she wasn't joking. Allington – who's more used to taking his car out two or three times a week with friends, or to the karaoke club he frequents on Saturday nights – couldn't conceive of 4.3 million people being together, never mind watching him.

'I just don't know,' he says when I ask him to explain why he thinks he's popular. 'I've never been popular like that in my life.' He gets a few cheers at the karaoke night, but nothing like this. He hits on a potential answer. 'I like people. I like to talk to people. I look at some of the comments and think: 'How nice.' I'm talking to people from all over the world, not just Birmingham where I am now.'

PART VI

GEOPOLITICS

29
GROWING POWER

TikTok expanded rapidly across the globe in 2019. While the company doesn't willingly share data about its user numbers unless really required, its usage is monitored by a mobile data and analytics provider, App Annie. And its findings were incredible. During 2019, users of Android smartphones outside China spent 68 billion hours – 7.8 million years – on TikTok. The rapid shutdown of the world instigated by the spread of the novel coronavirus from Wuhan in China in December that year proved even more of a boon for TikTok in 2020.

When the city of Wuhan, epicentre of the spread of Covid-19, was shut off from the outside world by order of the Chinese Central Communist Party on 23 January 2020, inhabitants of the city turned to their phones. The average smartphone user spent an extra five hours a day on their phones, and in total spent six hours a day on Douyin. A week and a half later, that had ballooned: the average Android smartphone user in China was spending 7.5 hours a day on Douyin, and more than three billion hours in total were spent on the app in a week – 130% more than the average week in 2019.

It was a pattern that would soon be repeated elsewhere. First Italy shut its borders and ordered its citizens to stay indoors on 9 March. Suddenly the average Italian spent an extra half an hour a day on their phones. Spain soon followed with stringent lockdown orders; they too lingered an extra 30 minutes a day on their mobiles. Not everyone turned to TikTok: plenty of other apps saw similar increases. But those who had heard about the news coverage, or had encountered their children or grandchildren tinkering around on the app just a few months earlier at Christmas family gatherings, suddenly had more time on their hands and curiosity to satisfy. So they logged onto their chosen app store, typed in the name, and hit download.

From January to March 2020, TikTok was the most downloaded app on Apple and Android worldwide. In that time, the number of monthly active users – an industry metric used to indicate people who opened up the app at least once a month – grew 45% in the United States. An extra 13 million people got hooked on TikTok across the United States, enough to fill a state the size of Illinois. In the same quarter in 2019, TikTok only added an extra two million users.

And once the users were there, they were there. Americans caught in TikTok's endless scroll spent 134 million hours on the app in March 2020 alone. Internal data shows that the average user opened the app at least eight times a day.

To get a sense of just how TikTok has come from seemingly nowhere, it's worth looking at its long-term growth. In March 2018, just months before the merger of Musical.ly and TikTok, users worldwide outside of China spent 66 million hours on the apps.

By March 2020, that had rocketed to 2.8 billion hours – or as much time as there has been between the Stone Age and today.

TikTok is already on a faster growth trajectory than YouTube, and more successful than Vine, its closest comparator. It's done so by being more addictive and immersive. If you want to watch a YouTube video, you have to seek it out. Increasingly, given the increasing length of the average video on the platform and the way in which YouTube viewing is shifting from phones and laptop screens to television sets in living rooms, you have to set aside a predetermined time to watch it. If you want to watch some TikToks, you simply open up the app and you're off, bathed in full-screen video and drowning in full-sound entertainment.

As well as being designed for addiction, TikTok is well-financed. ByteDance has spent more money than almost any other developer in history spreading TikTok across the globe. In 2019, it was spending $3 million a day on advertising in the United States to build up its audience. And it got lucky. TikTok could have been damaged by a freak event like coronavirus, but instead capitalised on it, becoming a haven for people looking for entertainment while stuck at home.

The app has grown not just in the number of users and the amount of time we spend on it, but also in the way it has seeped into the public consciousness. On 18 May 2019, the day after Lil Nas X's *Old Town Road* marked six weeks at the top of the Billboard Hot 100 chart, and a star-studded version of the music video was released on the internet, 21 stories were written about TikTok worldwide within 24 hours – less than one story every hour. A year later, on 18 May 2020, the day that TikTok announced it had poached Disney's head of streaming to become its chief executive in the United States, the number of stories written about TikTok was 990. On 18 May 2021, 1,430 separate stories were written, almost one a minute.

And it was starting to have an impact politically. Following the police killing of George Floyd in May 2020, social media inspired and galvanised the BlackLivesMatter protests in the US and around the world. TikTok was especially influential. Within a week of George Floyd's untimely death, 365,000 videos had been uploaded using the hashtag #BlackLivesMatter. The videos were seen 1.25 billion times. And George Floyd's name lived on through the app, as well as the protests. Within a week, 100,000 videos were posted in his name, which were seen 560 million times.

One of the videos that turned up on the evening of 30 May 2020 when you scrolled through the #BlackLivesMatter hashtag on TikTok came from Charli D'Amelio, at the age of 16 someone with intelligence and a maturity far beyond her years. The video, which took up the maximum amount of time allowable for a single TikTok, began: 'We, people of all colours, need to speak up at a time like this,' she said. 'As a person who has been given a platform to be an influencer, I realise with that title, I have a job to inform people on the racial inequalities of the world right now.'

That video, and the message it carried, was seen nearly 15 million times within 11 hours of being uploaded. Within 16 hours, it was seen more than 21 million times. D'Amelio was previously best known on the app for her intricately choreographed dance moves: how she danced dictated the next big trend on the app. But this was different. It wasn't hard to escape the fact that TikTok, which had long professed its apolitical viewpoint, was being compelled to take notice of the movement by its biggest star. Now it wasn't just what D'Amelio did that would shape the next trend on the app; what she said would dictate the types and tone of conversations in the days and weeks to come. TikTok, which had tried to present itself as studiously apolitical, was suddenly being dragged into the cultural and political conversation, and not just in the US.

30
INDIA BOOM
AND BUST

Few places took to TikTok in its early days like India. A rapidly expanding, increasingly connected population seeking snackable short-form entertainment and flush with the ability to access easy, roaming mobile internet data combined with TikTok in a powder keg explosion of interest.

After TikTok's September 2017 international launch, it took just six months for the app to be installed on one in every 20 smartphones in India. By April 2019, it took pride of place on the home screens of one in every four Indian phones, boosted by the roll-out of fast mobile connections by the telecommunications giant Jio. People living in India's tier 2 and 3 cities, which are smaller and less developed than its tier 1 giants such as Delhi, Bangalore, Chennai, Mumbai and Kolkata, took to the app in their droves as a diversion from their working lives.

More than half of TikTok's Indian users earnt less than 25,000 rupees, or $325, per month. It helped too that TikTok was among the first apps to use short, snackable video, not text, as its primary method of communication, a boon for users who are illiterate.

As well as documenting their everyday lives on the app through quirky videos, India's hundreds of millions of TikTok users followed key celebrities on the app, including Israil Ansari, who worked at a hardware store in Uttar Pradesh until his brother sent him a smartphone to try out TikTok, an app he had encountered when a friend showed him a snippet of a video at a wedding. The first video Ansari posted to TikTok was filmed in a paddy field in May 2018 by a passing 10-year-old boy who Ansari collared and asked to hold the phone. Ansari quickly gained followers. Aged 20, he had more than two million followers on the app; his videos, which reflected the quirky humour of India and made light of many of the country's curiosities for those trying to live in its system, were seen tens or hundreds of thousands of times.

Ansari exemplifies why TikTok gained such momentum in India. From a life of poverty in Uttar Pradesh, Ansari became a bona fide celebrity, stopped on the street by Mumbaikars who recognise him from the app. That's a relatively new development – at least, the admission of using TikTok out in the open.

For years TikTok was seen as something too gauche for the mega-rich in India's top cities, until the coronavirus kept the megacities' population indoors and Mumbaikars and other tier one city dwellers started adopting the app. In 2020, TikTok was used equally by those in Tier 1 cities and the sticks alike: 23 minutes a day. It got to the point of rivalling WhatsApp as the country's most popular app.

However, its growth had stirred controversy.

It started with two young women, performing handstands on the floor outside the temple, wearing baseball caps and skin tight jeans. Unsurprisingly, but disappointingly to custodians of the temple, the video that they posted to TikTok did not provide any details about the history or importance of Shah Jahān.

In the first half of the 17th century, the Mughal emperor of India waged war against a number of states on India's peninsula, winning Ahmadnagar, Golconda, Vijaypura and Kandahar in just two years between 1636 and 1638. He recognised that conquest wasn't enough, however. Just as quickly as he took land, others could seize it back, erasing his place in the history books. So he found another way to immortalise himself: by constructing buildings that would stand for centuries. In Agra, his capital for the first 20 years of his reign, he built two giant mosques, and the world's greatest monument to love: the Taj Mahal. Constructed over the course of 22 years, the Taj Mahal was an architecturally daring lament for Jahān's favourite wife, Mumtaz Mahal, who died during childbirth in 1631. In 1648, Jahān moved his capital 150 miles north from Agra to Delhi, and set about stamping his authority there. He built the Red Fort, one of Delhi's biggest tourist attractions, as well as another mosque, named the Jama Masjid.

Work started on the Jama Masjid two years after Jahān settled in Delhi. More than 5,000 workers heaved red sandstone and white marble up 30 steps to the building site for what was officially called the Masjid-i Jahānnumā, or world-displaying mosque. It took six years for labourers to build the structure, which faces Mecca and can hold 25,000 people for Friday prayers. More than 870,000 Indians, and another 125,000 tourists, traipse through its doors every year.

The cavalcade of tourists that visit the site alongside those on a pilgrimage will often take a few snaps for posterity or their social media – but the advent of TikTok in India added a new complication for Syed Ahmed Bukhari, the imam in charge of the mosque.

Posted to TikTok, the video of the two women in tight jeans performing handstands went viral in early 2019. What was designed by Jahān as a place of worship centuries before had become the picture-perfect backdrop for choreographed dances and super-viral social media posts.

The app said that it didn't endorse the video of the handstands, or a handful of other copycats who decided to use the historic building as a backdrop for their dancing. In fact it removed the video and other related ones. But people could download and repost them on other social platforms, ensuring they lived on in perpetuity.

The cavorting women continued to go viral on Facebook and Twitter, were the subject of intense media scrutiny in India, which suddenly had a new philosophical issue to consider: is a holy place the right location from which to plan your next viral success?

Bukhari had already made up his mind. 'Whether it's a mosque, or a temple, or a gurudwara, these places are for worship, not for singing and dancing,' he told The Telegraph newspaper in India. In May 2019, Bukhari asked its staff to begin monitoring people who came on the premises brandishing smartphones. They took to two electronic rickshaws, allowing them to traverse the entire grounds to stop any potential misdemeanours before they got out of hand.

One journalist asked Bukhari how he'd know whether someone was simply recording a video of the mosque to show their relatives – the 21st century equivalent of a holiday snap – or was planning a TikTok that would bring the holy shrine into disrepute. His answer was like that of United States Supreme Court Justice Potter Stewart when asked how to define pornography back in 1964: he'd know it when he saw it. Usually one person starts in front of the camera, and another enters the frame, dancing, jumping or doing something silly. 'This is when we know it's a TikTok video,' Bukhari protested.

At the same time, he knew that a team of stewards on electronic rickshaws wouldn't be enough to slow the spread of the super-viral social media app, three in every 10 downloads of which have come from India. So he commissioned a sign writer to daub stark white Hindi lettering on black wooden boards: 'जामा मस् जिद में तकिटोक की सख् तमनाही है'. Underneath, is an English translation: 'TikTok is strictly prohibited inside the mosque.' It was far from the only issue buffeting TikTok's popularity in India.

V Kalaiyarasan, a man from Chennai who had become TikTok famous for posting videos where he switched between male and female characters, killed himself in October 2018. The first flourishes of fame had turned sour, and so his family had turned against him, believing he had discredited their name. 'Many of his followers ridiculed him, calling him a transgender [sic] and a eunuch,' one of the police officers investigating his death on train tracks said.

V Kalaiyarasan was the first high-profile TikTok death, and hit at the heart of a problem for TikTok. To some, the content posted there was controversially pornographic in a conservative country such as India. TikTok sought to quell criticism from politicians and regulators by setting up data centres within India, a sop to those worried about its deleterious effect on the population. But it was not enough.

The backlash against TikTok began in Tamil Nadu in early 2019, where several local politicians jostled to ban the app, saying it was degrading culture. They succeeded in shutting down the app for two weeks. Then it spread to Madras, where a High Court banned the app in April 2019. The judgement said 'children who use the said application are vulnerable and [it] may expose them to sexual predators.' TikTok promised to clean up its act, and was unbanned in Madras later that month.

But the fast-growing app, which ByteDance claimed had lost $500,000 for every day it was banned in April 2019, was starting to take hits in the battle for its survival in the country.

It was censured by the national government that July for purported 'anti-national activities.' To ease concerns, TikTok launched an educational programme in the country. But it was an uneasy truce: the border deaths followed, as did the controversial content. A nine-second video posted by Faisal Siddiqui, a creator with 13 million subscribers on TikTok, made light of an acid attack. Siddiqui's account was quickly banned by TikTok, but repeated negative headlines meant the writing was on the wall.

On 29 June 2020, India's central government banned 59 Chinese apps, including TikTok, from the country. Every one of the apps, which were used by literally hundreds of millions of people in India, were 'prejudicial to [the] sovereignty and integrity of India, defence of India, security of state and public order,' the government claimed. Users who tried to open up TikTok in the country were met with a pop-up notice. 'Dear users,' it began. 'We are in the process of complying with the Government of India's directive to ban 59 apps. Ensuring the privacy and security of all our users in India remains our utmost priority.'

There was much, much more to it than that, of course. India was engaged in border skirmishes with China at the time. TikTok had been weaponised, its outlawing an attempt to stick it to the Chinese government and a jingoistic way to drum up national pride for a country worried about its territorial sovereignty. If it couldn't guarantee the shape of its country would remain the same, it could at least ensure that its internet was TikTok-free.

The government order was classified as an interim one, but TikTok never returned to the country. In January 2021, the interim ban was made permanent. By then, TikTok had lost at least 200 million users in India, who mostly scattered to homegrown competing apps that popped up in its place. None of them are much good – in polling for this book, just one in four Indians say the domestic alternatives are as good or better than the app they set out to replace. Around the same proportion – one in five – say they're worse.

While India was a big loss for TikTok, TikTok wasn't a big loss for India. Four in 10 Indians say their government was right to ban TikTok, compared to just 14% who say it was a bad idea. Roughly the same proportion are split as to whether they miss TikTok or not, with most saying they don't. And 37% say TikTok is a national security risk – perhaps because of geopolitics: half of Indians surveyed say they agreed TikTok was a Chinese-owned app.

For creators who had built up big followings, the ban was a blow. The family of Geetha Sridhar was receiving an income of around 50,000 rupees (£510) a month from brand sponsorships on videos in exchange for product placement. 'We kind of knew it was coming, so it wasn't a shock or disappointing,' says Sarada, her daughter. 'We knew some day this was going to happen.' Sarada had talked to some of her more tech-savvy friends, who warned her that the headlines against TikTok – which were swayed by a strong nationalist tint – signalled the end was nigh. One day

Sarada sat her mother down, a month before the ban came down in the middle of 2020, and they started posting on two different homegrown Indian platforms that vied to replace TikTok. They settled on two: Rizzle, and Chingari.

Rizzle became Geetha's favoured alternative. If she couldn't post to her near-million followers on TikTok, this would do. The problem was that the audience didn't always come with her. When we speak in early August 2020, a little over a month after TikTok shut down in India, Geetha has nearly 250,000 followers on Rizzle, who had watched her videos 10.4 million times. The rate of production had slowed: rather than dozens of quick videos on TikTok every day, Geetha had only done about a dozen in a month. 'It's hard, because it's not exactly like TikTok,' explains Sarada. 'And not a lot of people came directly from there, so we had to kind of start from scratch.'

But the audience that Geetha and her daughter had built up on TikTok did end up joining her – at least some of them. Rizzle's an okay alternative for her, but it doesn't have the two key elements we've already discovered make TikTok such a superpowered app: the amazing discovery algorithm that can transform an unprepossessing mother of two from India into an overnight star, and the easy creation tools that allow people like Geetha who perhaps aren't totally tech-literate to create videos that people want to watch.

Mother and daughter are also learning what it is that each app's audience wants. While Geetha's fans on TikTok lapped up the lockdown videos of the sari-clad mother dancing along to popular songs with a grin on her face, it appears – at least from the early trials she's been doing – that Rizzle's audience is much keener on simple cookery tips. It's been a frustrating process of trial and error for Geetha and Sarada. 'Slowly and steadily we're making videos and understanding what people like and don't,' says the daughter. 'We're seeing their response, then creating the content.'

31
END OF SILICON
VALLEY DOMINANCE

The rise of Chinese tech poses a direct challenge, not just to India but to the United States, whose Californian companies have so long dominated the internet.

We upload our lives to Facebook and to YouTube, which is owned by Google. We feel oddly comfortable sharing photos of our newborn babies, and documenting our lives in digital bread-crumbs to be pored over by their advertising algorithms. We trust that the Silicon Valley giants may exploit our data for monetary gain, but in so doing we won't come to harm. The data we share is still the same, a mixture of the banal that when taken in its totality ads up to something incredibly invasive. But instead of the address we're sending that data to be processed and analysed being Menlo Park, 94025 (the home of Facebook) or Mountain View, 94093 (the location of the Googleplex), we're sending it to a company whose headquarters is ShuangYuShu, Haidan Qu, Beijing. And some of us don't like that.

Now the power is ebbing away from the California enclave. Many believe that TikTok is just the the outrider for a Chinese invasion of tech. Hackles were raised at the American outpost of VidCon in 2019, when a semi-secretive, invite-only event called 'the East-West Forum' took place at the Marriott Hotel just down the road from the convention centre where the video conference was being held. The forum, organised by a group of Chinese tech giant executives tied to Qinteng University, happened on 17 July, the day before VidCon officially opened. It was, one attendee told journalist Taylor Lorenz, a way for Chinese tech company representatives to learn what issues creators and American tech firms had with their platforms. The event would prove to be an augur of the shift in power: viewed with hindsight, it was a scoping mission for Chinese companies looking to expand their reach to the West.

You only need to type in 'Is TikTok...' into Google to see some of the fears the most worried have. The search engine's algorithms – combing through our thoughts by tracking what we type into its search bar in just the same way as any other technology company – try and supply the answer it thinks we're most likely to want. Is TikTok safe, dangerous, bad, haram, and Chinese are among the top search results.

That's fuelled by broader issues than a video sharing app where people clown about. But if TikTok continues its unparalleled rise, then they are questions that could become moot because it'd be the first of many Chinese apps coming to wrest control of our smartphone screens. And tech's biggest names know that – and have done for a while. In October 2018, Tim Cook, the head of Apple, stopped by ByteDance's headquarters while on a visit to Beijing, part of regular business overseeing the business's growth in China. He wanted to get an idea of what life was like at the company, that at the time was starting to spin up its growth to near-stratospheric levels. As he walked around the ByteDance office floor, glad handing grinning employees who had their smartphones up to their face to capture the presence of the well-known chief executive in their offices, Yiming Zhang walked alongside him. Little did the world know that in a matter of years the pair could feasibly switch places and no one would bat an eyelid.

ByteDance isn't the first Chinese company to expand outside the country's borders – Tencent, which runs the WeChat messaging app, tried to do so in 2014 with little success, because users were already hooked on WhatsApp and Facebook Messenger. But ByteDance is far and away the most successful.

Some of the fears that people have outlined – that decisions on product direction and features are centralised in ByteDance's Chinese offices, for instance, or that the company's satellite offices around the world focus more on operational decisions – aren't unique to ByteDance. Look at Facebook or Apple or Netflix or Amazon. Practically every technology company develops its software as a one-size-fits-all product to be used around the world, and deals with the small amount of friction that results by having staff smooth over issues with local governments worldwide. That's also what happens with TikTok: until it recently cleaved its company in two, putting up more of a distinct firewall between China and the rest of the world, the majority of TikTok's features were cribbed from Douyin, and developed by the coding team in China.

What differs is that there's a general discomfort about that, because of the broader geopolitical baggage that comes with having a Chinese-focused company dominating the tech landscape. What ByteDance is doing is no different from any other company. What is different is where it's based, and the governmental system under which it operates. Fears are fuelled either by xenophobia or a justified wariness of the reach and goals of the tentacles of the

Chinese state, depending on which side of the argument you sit on. Is ByteDance a stealthy attempt for the Chinese state to exert soft power over the whole planet? An attempt to extract data underneath the guise of toned, tanned teenagers dancing along to their favourite pop songs? Or is it just a company trying to build its brand and bolster its business – far from a communist con, a capitalist triumph, trying to shunt its way onto the same playing field as the likes of Google, Apple and Facebook, whom we hold up as examples of American success and the opportunities of the free market?

Is Yiming Zhang a puppet of the Chinese state, cowed and willing to cede to their demands, crafting an app – and behind it, a bigger company offering a range of products – that's designed to shift perceptions of China in the West and smooth the path for the country to become the dominant superpower? Or is he a small town dreamer who had big ideas that he got from voraciously reading the stories of American exceptionalism in business biographies that lionise success? A person trying to make the world a happier place, and to make himself richer in the process?

These are all questions that you likely have strong opinions on either way. The character sketch biography of Zhang would indicate that it's the latter, rather than the former: he has lofty goals, and unusually prescient and far-ranging vision. He's eager, despite growing up in a country uniquely designed to limit aspirations to within its border and political system, to break out of that and to bring joy to the world. But many people don't, and won't, believe that. They have their own feelings, backed up by various forms of evidence, of variable quality. Public sentiment doesn't agree with my stance: 67% of Americans today feel cold towards China, up from 46% in 2018. That's a staggering increase, not least given it's bookended perfectly by the rise of TikTok, the Chinese-born app that brings more happiness to so many.

The strength of feeling is why the future path of TikTok, and behind it, ByteDance, matters so much. Because viewpoints are so entrenched on either side of the divide, the success or failure of a relatively inconsequential app when looked at in the grand scheme of things has become a test of the future power balance of the entire planet. And the foot soldiers on either side of the argument are willing to defend their thoughts to the hilt – because they see it either as a tamping down of the free market, or a mortal peril to the status quo and a potential descent into a world they've spent the last 70 years or more trying to avoid.

32
OPPOSITION GROWS
IN THE UNITED STATES

What Yiming Zhang and Alex Zhu can't possibly have known when they set up their short-form video sharing apps in the mid-2010s is the way in which their popularity would increase tensions between East and West. In many ways, the row over TikTok isn't about the future of the tech sector for the next 25 years and who controls it, but also about the future direction of the world.

China's president Xi Jinping announced the Belt and Road Initiative in 2013. It's seen by the ruling party in China as a way to 'embrace a brighter future' by enhancing connections between China and the rest of the world. But to sino-sceptics in governments across the globe, it's a way for China to exercise soft power, and to shift the centre of global control away from Washington and London to Beijing.

It's an issue played out at various levels across the planet. In skirmishes over borders where China abuts India, with troops starting to cross the boundaries into another nation's territory. In fears about integrating Chinese-made technology into key communication systems, with governments across the globe engaged in torturous debate about whether to allow Huawei to run their previous 5G mobile internet networks – or to limit the company's oversight. In tariff wars between a belligerent US President who wanted to get one over on China, threatening to cut off ties with the superpower best placed to supplant the United States as the world's leader.

Indeed, TikTok had been on the radar of US authorities long before Donald Trump took a dislike to the app. Its merger with Musical.ly between 2017 and 2018 first caused problems for the new super app that would eventually lead to a $5.7 million fine from the US Federal Trade Commission for violating children's privacy. But it was how it intended to deal with all users' privacy that first alarmed the China-sceptic US senators Charles Schumer and Tom Cotton.

A cross-party consensus was reached by the senators, who in October 2019 asked the Office of the Director of National Intelligence to investigate TikTok's willingness to say no if compelled to give up Western users' data by the Chinese government. 'China's vague patchwork of intelligence, national security, and cybersecurity laws compel Chinese companies to support and cooperate with intelligence work controlled by the Chinese Communist Party,' the senators wrote. 'Without an independent judiciary to review requests made by the Chinese government for data or other actions, there is no legal mechanism for Chinese companies to appeal if they disagree with a request.' TikTok denied then, as it does now, ever handing over data to the Chinese government.

Things spiralled from there. The Committee on Foreign Investment in the United States (CFIUS), which reviews business deals involving international companies investing in the US, opened a national security investigation into TikTok's purchase of Musical.ly within a week or so of the senators' letter.

By December 2019, the US Navy had banned its personnel from using TikTok because of security fears.

A consensus, fuelled by the America-first right wing of the Republican party and its China hawks, was growing against TikTok: the app was no good, and its existence was a danger to American values. Josh Hawley, a reactionary Republican grooming himself as Donald Trump's spiritual successor, who has since written a book railing against big tech, co-authored legislation to ban TikTok from any device issued by the US government. 'TikTok is a major security risk to the United States, and it has no place on government devices,' Hawley said as he tabled the bill in March 2020.

Among China hawks in Washington, the anti-TikTok campaign in the United States was gaining a head of steam. The Trump administration largely stayed out of the squabble until users of the app embarrassed the president by buying up vast numbers of tickets to one of his presidential campaign events then not turning up. For a notoriously tetchy leader concerned about his public image, it was a major insult – and one that TikTok the business played no real role in.

On 6 July 2020, a week to the day after India announced it was banning TikTok alongside 58 other Chinese-made apps, then US Secretary of State Mike Pompeo appeared on the Fox News programme the Ingraham Angle, hosted by Laura Ingraham.

Pompeo, who for little over a year was the director of the CIA before being the US's representative abroad, covered a handful of topics in the interview, but was asked by Ingraham in the final few moments of the segment whether, given India's ban and Australia's worry, the United States should be considering, right now, tonight, a ban on TikTok.

'We're certainly looking at it,' Pompeo shot back, reassuring the Republican-supporting viewers of Fox News that their safety was paramount. 'I don't want to get out in front of the president, but it's something we're looking at,' he added.

Ingraham, bringing the interview to an end, wanted something more. 'Would you recommend that people download that app on their phones tonight, tomorrow, anytime currently?' she asked. Pompeo replied: 'Only if you want your private information in the hands of the Chinese Communist Party.'

It was enough to send Republicans into raptures, and to chill the spirits of those who had been trying to build a base of popularity on TikTok – many of them Americans who supported Trump. In group chats on Telegram and Discord, two popular apps to talk with like-minded people, TikTokers of all sizes worried about an imminent ban. When Donald Trump quickly confirmed the US was mulling over a total and complete shutdown of TikTok in another TV interview, anxieties rose further. They had seen their Indian counterparts lose their livelihoods and entertainment outlets during a lockdown, and worried they were to follow.

Those within the industry supporting TikTok creators found their inboxes deluged with emails from the talent themselves, from their agents and their managers, trying to map out the potential ramifications. Should they try and shift their audience off the app onto American competitors? Should they follow what looked to be the prevailing school of thought and actually delete the app? Others were more angry than anxious: they'd seen the president's statement, and that of his secretary of state. Should they still support the app if what was being said about its ties to the central communist party was true? How could they still support it?

Those worries only got worse when an email pinged into the inboxes of Amazon's 500,000 employees at 5:16pm London time on 10 July. Its subject line? 'Action required: Mandatory removal of TikTok by 10-Jul.'

'Hello,' the email began. 'Due to security risks, the TikTok app is no longer permitted on mobile devices that access Amazon email. If you have TikTok on your device, you must remove it by 10-Jul to retain mobile access to Amazon email. At this time, using TikTok from your Amazon laptop browser is allowed.'

The email landed in inboxes just as Amazon's staff on the West Coast of the United States were waking up. Shortly after lunchtime, after a social media storm erupted trying to decipher why one of Silicon Valley's big beasts was taking such a definitive line on the new Chinese tech incursion, things got stranger. 'This morning's email to some of our employees was sent in error,' an Amazon spokesperson sheepishly told reporters. 'There is no change to our policies right now with regard to TikTok.'

Then Donald Trump surprised everyone.

33
DONALD
TRUMP ACTS

Air Force One was at cruising altitude when Donald Trump came back to meet the press corps on his way to a campaign rally in Florida at the end of July 2020. The president had taken off from Washington DC earlier that day and given a brief soundbite to the media assembled to see him off: he planned to ban TikTok. But this was Donald Trump, a man who says one thing and means the other, for whom lies roll off the tongue as readily as truths. No one really thought he meant it; he'd get bored of pursuing TikTok and move on to something else.

Until he meant it.

It was late in the evening of 31 July when Trump came into the rear cabin, where White House reporters who follow the president around were corralled. He wanted to clarify things: he wasn't blustering. 'As far as TikTok is concerned, we're banning them from the United States,' he said. 'I have that authority. I can do it with an executive order,' he added, also saying he could also use emergency economic powers if necessary.

With just a handful of words, Trump was planning to ban an entertainment option popular with 100 million Americans. An executive order in August 2020 gave TikTok an execution date 45 days hence unless it sold up to an American partner.

China's state news service, widely believed to be the voice of the government, called the demanded fire sale of TikTok 'dirty and unfair and based on bullying and extortion.' In the meantime, TikTok's US lawyers played a strategic game of kicking the can down the road, delaying the imposition of any ban by the US administration until after the impending US presidential election. The gamble seemed to be that if Donald Trump went away, so would the problem. In late August TikTok and ByteDance both had sued Donald Trump and his Secretary of Commerce, Wilbur Ross, for unconstitutionally trying to ban the app just three days earlier. The lawsuit also claimed what many in TikTok had been saying privately for months: that the Trump administration, no stranger to doing things they want despite decades of established norms, had trampled over what was meant to be an apolitical investigation by the Committee on Foreign Investment in the United States into the app and forced it to reach a conclusion against TikTok.

That was the second lawsuit Trump would face over TikTok that week: a technical programme manager working at the company out of its Mountain View, California office, Patrick Ryan, worried that the executive orders Trump announced would put him out of a job and make TikTok unable to legally pay him. Indeed, in his lawsuit, Ryan claimed that's exactly what the company told him: that it worried it would be breaching the terms of the executive order if it paid its 1,500 US-based employees. It was a concern for Ryan, who joined the company from Google in March 2020. It was a concern for other employees, who were posting anxious questions in Lark, TikTok's internal communication system. Vanessa Pappas, the US managing director, reassured workers worried about their future.

Then something bigger happened. It was announced in late August that Kevin Mayer, the clean-cut former Disney executive who had only joined TikTok as its chief executive in May, was leaving the company. The geopolitical situation Mayer found himself in was untenable, he told employees in a letter announcing his departure. 'I have done significant reflection on what the corporate structural changes will require, and what it means for the global role I signed up for.' When he accepted the job in May, Mayer expected not only to be the chief executive of TikTok's United States arm – which was de facto in charge of every aspect of the app outside of China – but also the chief operating officer of ByteDance, TikTok's parent company. It was a prestigious role in two companies that were coming to dominate the world.

Three months later, he was looking at a future away from ByteDance as the Chinese company strove to build a wall between its core offices and those in the United States, and becoming a middle manager in the event that a buyer wanted to keep him but place its own people in charge. Within a matter of months Mayer's potential fiefdom had gone from overseeing nearly 700 million users and tens of thousands of employees to one around one-seventh that size. It was a chastening experience. It was also worrying for the man who many thought was joining TikTok to bide his time until he could become head of Disney.

Yiming Zhang recognised Mayer's difficulty, saying: 'I fully understand the resulting outcome that we land upon due to the political circumstances we are operating within could have significant impact on his job in any scenario, but particularly given his global role while he's based in the US.'

While murmurings on Lark, the company's internal communication system, were quiet in China, apart from the odd worker hypothesising that the decision was perhaps a one guided by personal ambition for the future, workers elsewhere were more outspoken. Employees within the US office were aghast at the news. 'I am shocked but I understand,' said one worker in the trust and safety team.

It was the latest buffeting for the app and its underlying business in a torrid year. At the same time as TikTok was achieving extraordinary success, it was living through a nightmare. Rank-and-file employees feared for their futures, while the executives tasked with running a business successfully – already a difficult enough task when it was growing so fast, during a pandemic – were now being asked to massage the ego of politicians.

During the second half of 2020, Trump's Democratic opponent in the presidential election, Joe Biden, refused to campaign in person due to the coronavirus. Trump was spoiling for an opponent and hit upon an ideal one to distract from his failures: TikTok. Within a five-day period in midsummer, Trump's campaign saturated Facebook and Instagram with more than 450 political ads claiming 'TikTok is spying on you.' In that period, the messages, which were interspersed with images of soldiers in Chinese military uniforms, were seen by more than 5.5 million Americans. If Joe Biden wasn't going to contest the election, Donald Trump was going to make it a race to the White House between him and Yiming Zhang.

TikTok, and its executive team, quickly became public enemy number one in the eyes of many Americans. In August, rumours ping-ponged around the future of the app. Microsoft was about to swoop in to save the app, and the deal to buy the company's American operations would close by mid-September. Within a day, Trump appeared to give his assent to the deal, but then threw a spanner in the works. Signing a separate executive order behind a desk in the White House, the president was asked about a TikTok-Microsoft deal. Mid-ramble, he said something that bordered on extortion. 'I said a very substantial portion of that price is going to have to come into the Treasury of the United States,' he told reporters, comparing it to a landlord-tenant relationship. Without that cut – and the US Treasury getting 'a lot of money, a lot of money' – Trump wouldn't sign off on the deal. The proclamation puzzled many, and days later TikTok filed its lawsuit while another bidder entered the fray: Oracle, a software company better known by straight-suited businessmen, whose chairman Larry Ellison was a noted Republican donor.

By September, with Microsoft questioning why it would give a kickback to the Trump administration, Oracle became TikTok's preferred buyer. Oracle and ByteDance even announced a deal – but they contradicted each other about its terms. Oracle said that it would wholly own TikTok's US operations in Texas, and suggested that the US supermarket Walmart would be part of the deal. Not so fast, said ByteDance: it believed it would still own an 80% stake in what it was calling 'TikTok Global,' suggesting the US operations and those in the rest of the world outside China would stay together.

Donald Trump had heard something different from both. According to the US president, TikTok would fund a $5 billion education fund – which was a surprise to ByteDance.

TikTok kept fighting its legal action, and successive judges in the cases largely agreed with it that the demanded fire sale didn't seem to follow due order. TikTok was allowed to kick the can down the road time and time again. Despite the repeated twists and turns, in the end, it didn't even matter.

In November, Trump lost the US presidential election; in January, he lost power. The world woke up and wondered if the last four years had been a bad dream. But those within TikTok weren't so ready to call an end to the war with the US government, and with good reason, as we'll see shortly.

TikTok gained a new permanent CEO, Singaporean Shouzi Chew, in April 2021 – perhaps the clearest indication yet that those in charge of the app felt that the American problem had mostly gone away. Chew's appointment was an attempt to steady the ship after nearly a year of storms. Where he was based was also significant. At one point, TikTok looked like it wanted to base its business outside China in the US, but Trump's hostility ended that. While the company said it hadn't yet decided where to locate its global headquarters, it has taken out big office spaces in Singapore, and headcount there is rising, including for its new software technology division called BytePlus.

TikTok still lives on in the US, though its reputation there has been damaged by Donald Trump's attacks. A third of Americans think TikTok is a national security risk, according to exclusive polling commissioned for this book. Six in 10 say it's a Chinese-owned app, half don't trust TikTok to look after their personal data, and half think TikTok might share their data with the Chinese government.

So what is the truth?

34
DIGGING
INTO THE DATA

Stoked by a raft of stories of Western apps invasively tracking personal data, and amplified by fears that apps of Chinese origin are more likely to use subterfuge, the most sceptical TikTok users and wary politicians fear TikTok is a giant data hoover. The fear, they say, is that every last piece of information about you is collected both within and outside the app, then sent back to China for processing.

There, the most fearful about TikTok say, it could theoretically be handed over to the Chinese state, under whose thumb any company in the country operates.

TikTok's Western representatives have repeatedly said they haven't been asked to hand over the data of those in the West, and wouldn't even if they were asked. China watchers worry that's misrepresenting a state request to see data as a conversation, rather than a fait accompli.

Yet there remains no evidence that TikTok has handed over, or would hand over, data on individual Western users to authorities in China, and repeated analyses by cybersecurity experts of the app's code show little to differentiate the type and volume of data it collects on its users from any of the apps we happily use every day.

There also seems little danger in Chinese spies seeing what songs teenagers dance along to, or any other information that could be identified from an individual user's use of the app. Little information about national security levels or relations between the East and West can be gleaned from glancing inside a suburban American teenager's bedroom for up to 60 seconds at a time. (However, it's true that changes when you're talking about the teenage children of Western politicians, some of whom are on the app despite the potential risks that could result. TikTok-literate journalists, for instance, knew about the UK's plans for coronavirus and the health and wellbeing of major cabinet ministers by following the daughter of Conservative politician Michael Gove on the app.) The most personal information likely to be of use to those trying to hack into our devices, such as bank accounts, web browsing and personal communications, aren't even tracked or gathered by TikTok.

In all this it's crucial to recognise that the debate around TikTok's use of user data sits within a wider context, which includes Western concern about the rise of China and, in particular, the use of its technology in the West. If this one app can gain so much sway among hundreds of millions of citizens, the Western thinking goes, what else could come around the corner? It helps to explain some of the robust responses to TikTok from various seats of power, and the backlash it has faced from frenzied sections of those countries' populations. When you look at the fervour with which a nationwide campaign to boycott TikTok gathered speed across India in the first half of 2020, it's worth remembering that it happened at the same time as a month-long standoff between Indian and Chinese troops over a disputed border in the Himalayas which led to bloodshed. That campaign led to TikTok's star rating on app stores tanking to 1.2 stars after millions of negative ratings. Its place in app store rankings – based on the number of downloads it received – dropped significantly. (In the end, Google removed eight million one-star ratings it believed were maliciously posted.)

So, too, could Donald Trump's campaign against TikTok be seen through the lens of a US president looking to demonise an enemy to bolster his chances of re-election after his plan to run on revitalising the economy faded, rather than because of evidence of any data danger. TikTok has arguably become the fall guy in a superpower battle that looks set to define the future of our world for decades. In 2010, when US-Chinese relations were warmer, with a more measured president sat behind the famed Resolute desk, the Committee on Foreign Investment in the United States (CFIUS) reviewed 93 inward investment deals – six of which were from China. By 2017, the number of transactions CFIUS was asked to investigate had risen to 237 – including 60 by Chinese companies. From Chinese firms being at the centre of one in 20 investigations under Barack Obama's presidency, they were suddenly the focus of one in four under Donald Trump.

Concern at the rise of Chinese tech hasn't been confined to the borders of the United States. There's been disquiet in the UK, Europe and Australia, too. Politicians there are worried about granting Huawei too great access to the country's telecommunications system, and is steadfastly refusing to allow untrammelled access to 5G networks. It's the reason that the European Union opened an investigation into TikTok's data practices, and why representatives of the company were hauled up in front of politicians in the UK and Australia, where they were quizzed about the company's ties to China, and what they would do if they received a tap on the shoulder and a request to hand over user data to Beijing.

One high-ranking Western politician, who is far from a friend of China, told me they didn't think TikTok was a deep state plot to poison the well. But they did worry that the use of artificial intelligence-powered video analysis was potentially being used to track Uyghur Muslims. 'ByteDance is doing deals with groups that are genuinely persecuting people,' they told me. 'That's a problem. It's not TikTok: it's ByteDance.' TikTok's UK director of government relations and public policy strongly rebutted these claims at a parliamentary hearing on behalf of its parent company. 'I can unequivocally deny the allegations,' said Elizabeth Kanter. 'ByteDance Ltd nor any of its subsidiaries produce, operate or disseminate any sort of surveillance equipment. The company does not have any personnel related to surveillance, so those allegations are false.'

Chinese firms are keen to change the narrative away from being part of an overbearing China towards being good corporate citizens. Ren Zhengfei, founder of Huawei, has tried to quell unrest about his company's access to the world's 5G networks – and the data that's transmitted over them, some of which is likely crucial to national security – by engaging in a so-called 'marshmallow campaign' of positive PR stories. Huawei contributed to the United States' battle against coronavirus by donating masks, gloves and gowns to New York, one of the areas worst-hit by Covid-19. At the same time, it's loaded its British board with reputable, recognisable names from UK business who have previously worked at some of the biggest companies in the West.

TikTok and ByteDance's decisions to make splashy donations in support of the fight against coronavirus may be seen as similar decisions – as could its tendency to hire executives from Disney and other blue-chip companies that represent the red, white and blue beating heart of Americana. Indeed, looking from the outside in – and with eyes and ears on the ground – it almost seems like the company behind TikTok is reimagining itself to try to satisfy the requirements of Western policymakers.

By hiring local executives with knowledge of the market and building out the competencies of its in-country teams, TikTok's developers have been trying to extend the distance between Beijing and the apps used around the world to allay the fears of those most concerned about its impact. The internal communications, which saw many decisions being fed back to Beijing for a final action, have instead been moored within individual countries.

According to insiders, internal data on TikTok employees has since been firewalled off from access from employees in Beijing in an attempt to draw a distinction between the controlling company and the individual apps on a country level. ByteDance knows that its connections to China and its origins from the country could prove problematic to those who believe the app to be a ruse to siphon off Western users' data for the Chinese Communist Party. So it has been working in earnest to make sure no one can say information is being transferred to China. 'The strategy for the company has always been a separation of what happens in China from the rest of the world,' one high-ranking executive explained to me.

The UK and US heads of TikTok have been clear: no user data is transferred to the Chinese government, and no data would be if asked. European and United States' user data ends up in a data centre in Virginia, with a backup in Singapore. European users' data will soon be transferred instead to Dublin, where the app is building a trust and safety centre opening in 2022.

However, when you are running an international tech empire, not everything is always so clear-cut. The reality is that while explicitly identifiable user data isn't transferred to China, and external third parties are welcome to come in and analyse the data flows to prove there's no access, some data is sent back to ByteDance headquarters. Two TikTok employees, working in two different locations, told me on two separate occasions during 2020 that some data did, of course, make its way to ByteDance engineers in China. It's something the company confirmed in a blog post published in August 2020 that gained little attention: engineers based in China would of course get access to some data, but in a highly controlled way.

The engineers aren't siphoning off personal data on what videos you're watching of the type Taha Shakil shared with me, allowing an insight into your day-to-day lives. But they are accessing data nonetheless. They're doing it to spot things like bot attacks and to check whether the algorithm they've coded is functioning as intended. Where there is any access, I was told, it's done in a scrutinised way with a third party ensuring nothing can be taken. Roland Cloutier, a former member of the U.S. Air Force, Department of Defense, and Department of Veterans Affairs, and TikTok's chief security officer since April 2020, maintained that the company's access management plan to user data was robust. He said: 'We have stringent security control, data defence and access assurance technologies in place, [as well as] encryption in place.' Some employees are given time-limited access to data in order to do their job, then their access is revoked. Yet Cloutier wouldn't tell me how many ByteDance employees had access to that data when I asked him in June 2021. He wouldn't even tell me whether it was tens, hundreds, thousands – or tens of thousands of ByteDance's 100,000-strong workforce.

Another employee told me how user data from Western countries, including personal identifying data, is regularly transferred into spreadsheets that are shared around TikTok using ByteDance's internal messaging system, Lark, called Feishu in China – at least some of the servers for which are based in China. 'We have these very inconsistent statements now around what we're trying to accomplish, and we don't necessarily have a policy,' they said.

The reality here is that there is no big con, but instead a little white lie. It's understandable why it's happened: the geopolitical situation is so tense that for TikTok to admit the reality – that some data ends up in China, because that's where its engineering base is, even if it's obscured and tightly controlled – would risk setting off a firestorm of controversy.

There are, however, sometimes legitimate questions about the treatment of personal user data by big tech companies, including Facebook but also ByteDance. There have been instances where data has been not hacked – where data is illicitly obtained by breaching a company's security systems, presumably for malicious reasons – but 'scraped' from accessible information, agglomerated and dumped in a corner of the internet. One such scrape involved Douyin, TikTok's Chinese sibling (there is no evidence that TikTok is affected). It hasn't been previously reported until this book's publication.

Personal data points from 479,000 users of Douyin, dating back a number of years, were found on a publicly accessible computer server and passed to me in late 2020. Among the users are at least 89 people resident in the United Kingdom and 287 in the United States.

The data contains personal identifiable information (PII) about users, such as birthdays and location. Such information is given freely by users to Douyin but is not displayed to the general public in a user's profile. Such information is obviously not the most serious that can be obtained from app users, such as credit card details or passwords which can be used to swindle or blackmail members of the public. Nonetheless, some users may be surprised that information not on their public profiles had been made available to web users en masse, if they knew where to look.

Of the British Douyin contingent, for instance, one was a young Chinese woman, born in 1995, whose profile photo showed her with a flash of bright red lipstick and a prominent fringe, wearing a dramatic white hood over her head. Douyin had identified her location as England, and specifically London. Her gender was recorded in the app's code as '2' – a woman, and the data indicated she was more a consumer than a creator. Her 'selfVideoCount' in the data was just three, while she had favourited a total of 6,926 videos on the app.

She was one of many (I am withholding data such as usernames that could pinpoint an individual user). In the United States was a 20-year-old living in Glendale, California with an anime-style avatar. At the time the data was posted onto a public internet server, they had 2,930 followers and 2,871 following them. Their 'awemeCount', an indication of their perceived popularity on the app by ByteDance, was 27. But they were a power user of Douyin, liking 83,000 videos in total.

ByteDance was approached about the scrape of Douyin user details for this book. It declined to comment.

CREATOR FOCUS
MACKENZIE TURNER

Name: Mackenzie Turner
Username: @mackenzieturner0
Following: 158
Followers: 4.1M
Likes: 112.3M
Speciality: Comedy skits

As the car wound through downtown Vancouver on the way to a hotel, Sham Faek was laying out everything he had learned as a result of his online fame. Faek, a 23-year-old Canadian who was the child-hood sweetheart of Lael Hansen, another big YouTuber, was chatting to Hansen's longtime friend, Mackenzie Turner, and her boyfriend, Kobe Zhou.

The group had known each other since high school, and had watched as Faek and Hansen's lives had been transformed by Instagram and YouTube, which had given them an audience of millions. Turner and Zhou had helped them along the way, appearing in videos whenever needed, and spending long days and nights meticulously packing up merchandise that fans had bought.

Turner wanted to follow in their footsteps. She had set up a YouTube channel in 2017 but by her own admission, wasn't a great vlogger. 'I wasn't very comfortable in front of the camera,' she recalled. 'I was nervous and shy, so my videos didn't come across as great.' She decided to try TikTok, taking advantage of the fact that she didn't have to be engaging for minutes, but instead for seconds. Faek and Hansen encouraged her, saying TikTok would be a good way to try out social media – and besides, it was the hot new app. If you were going to ride a bike with stabilisers, you might as well make it a motorbike.

The day before she posted her first video, Faek advised Turner how to get over her awkwardness on camera. 'He told me not to be scared because the biggest thing that stops people from doing anything on social media is being nervous or scared of what other people are going to think about you,' Turner said. 'He's like: "Who cares what anyone else thinks? You have to go full force into it and need to be posting every single day".'

Turner posted her first video the next day – a skit where she gets into an argument with her dad for asking him to take part in a TikTok as he cleans the kitchen. Within a month of joining TikTok in July 2019, she had her first viral post. She was also getting better at feeling at ease on camera – a side effect of posting several videos a day to the platform. 'I was hooked on it,' she admits. 'I was addicted, and wanted to get better and create better content as I went on.'

Turner made a name for herself among an audience of young girls who lapped up her girly, quirky, outlandish content. Now she wasn't just supporting her friends, shoving T-shirts into boxes and bags but building up her own audience – which stands 4.1 million-strong on TikTok. The majority are female, and a self-reported poll found the core component was aged nine to 12 years old. 'Doing fun, girly videos is definitely the style they love,' she said.

Success has allowed Turner and her boyfriend to move into a new apartment, with two bedrooms and a den, just down the street from where she grew up. It's the first time she's moved out of her parents' home. One of the bedrooms and the den have been turned over to Turner's burgeoning career as a digital creator. The second bedroom is a vanity room and where she films some of her content, while the den has a desk with two computer screens where Zhou edits his girlfriend's videos.

Keeping up with audience demands for content on various apps is now a full-time job, which is why Turner paused her schooling at Simon Fraser University, putting her plans to become a teacher on hold. It wasn't what her parents wanted. 'As I like to tell my Mom, we take breaks, we don't drop out,' she said. 'Dropping out means you failed. Taking a break doesn't.' The decision was partly motivated by the fame Turner was finding on TikTok. She began to recognise things weren't normal when she was stopped at a Christmas party at the gym where she worked as a personal trainer. A young girl and her mother came running up to her at a bowling alley asking if they could take a picture with her.

The job takes up six days a week. Turner and Zhou wake up at 8am and go to the gym for an hour. When they get back, Turner will get ready, do her make up and hair, and start filming videos. Twice a week she spends the day filming for YouTube; the other days she focuses on TikTok, starting at 9am and finishing around 6pm. She can film four TikTok videos in a day, planning out skits and conceits and bringing them to fruition. In the time Turner is on camera, Zhou is next door, editing the YouTube videos.

Despite her success, Turner still feels vulnerable. She started her YouTube channel after advice from her friends. 'Everyone is kind of nervous because Vine just disappeared and died so quickly after many people got famous,' she said. 'The smart ones on Vine took their career and built a huge platform for themselves on YouTube.'

PART VII

THE FUTURE

35
COMPETITION

Ask the uninitiated and they may tell you TikTok is the spiritual or literal successor to Vine, the Twitter-owned short-form video app. (That's actually Byte, the short-form app developed by Vine's creator Dom Hofman after a three-year hiatus, which was released to the public with a whimper just before Christmas 2019.) But while TikTok ran where Vine walked, plenty of ByteDance's competitors have spotted TikTok's success and want to have a piece of the action.

It's the reason why Facebook released Lasso in November 2018. It's also probably why Facebook tried again in May 2020 with another app, called Collab, that borrows heavily from TikTok's aesthetic. And it's part of the reason why an unusual video app called Zynn surged up the app stores in the same month. Subtitled 'Fun way to reward yourself,' Zynn looks eerily like TikTok. Except it's playing ByteDance at its own game. It's paying users. Open up the app for the first time and a graphical representation of a wrapped and bowed present pops up at the bottom of the screen, giving you 500 points, the in-app currency that can be redeemed eventually for money. One point is one ten thousandth of a dollar. But there are bigger cash rewards on offer: you can get $6 into your account for recommending a friend to download the app and engage with Zynn's content. If they keep engaging with the content for the next two days, another $2 will be credited to your balance.

Zynn is owned by a company called Owlii, which was bought by a Chinese firm called Kuaishou. The company's app Kwai is Douyin's biggest competitor in China. While Douyin has 600 million users logging on every day, Kwai can lay claim to 480 million in China. And just as Douyin gave birth to TikTok, Kwai has given birth to Zynn. 'Zynn is a product we tailor made for the North American market,' a spokesperson for Owlii told tech website The Information. And in a sense of the fight Owlii was willing to put up against ByteDance, the spokesperson added: 'We believe short video is far from over.'

The threat isn't an empty one. While ByteDance has extensive cash reserves, Kuaishou has deep pockets, too. It raised $2 billion in December 2019 from a number of investors, including Tencent, with which ByteDance has been competing in China. It even launched a blockbuster initial public offering (IPO) in Hong Kong in February 2021, which valued Kuaishou at $180 billion.

Kuaishou and ByteDance are locked in a war for users, and engage in sneaky tactics to swipe them from each other – which explains the pay-for-play model that Zynn is utilising in the United States. Frequently, such tussles have ended up in court. Tencent has previously sued ByteDance for infringing its copyright and operating unfair competition. Baidu, China's version of Google, has also sued ByteDance for 'interfering' with search results to promote Toutiao. And Kuaishou and ByteDance have traded dates in court for a variety of different reasons. In March 2020, ByteDance petitioned the Beijing Haidan District People's

Court to rule in its favour, claiming that Kuaishou was gaming search engine results on app stores, showing people its products when they searched for ByteDance apps. In exchange, Kuaishou has dragged ByteDance to court in Beijing, saying that it's hijacking search results when anyone searches for 'Kuaishou' on app stores in China, presenting them with the opportunity to download ByteDance apps instead. It was 'unfair competition,' claims Kuaishou, and ByteDance ought to pay Kuaishou five million yuan in compensation – around $700,000.

More damaging to TikTok's future in the West than a fellow Chinese competitor are two US-based rivals, one of whom is keen to snap at TikTok's heels, while the other towers over the app, even with its massive userbase.

Triller likes to style itself as the ethical alternative to TikTok. It was set up by Mike Lu, a passionate restaurateur and a serial tech founder. Major musicians took a stake in Triller and offered up the rights to their music to be used on it legally – an issue TikTok had long wrestled with. As rumours of a ban on TikTok swirled, Triller signed a number of major TikTokers, including Josh Richards, co-founder of TalentX Entertainment, as executives. They brought along creators like Noah Beck, the talented footballer turned social media sensation. Richards signed on to the company by saying that he had joined Triller 'after seeing the US and other countries' governments' concerns over TikTok.' However, he and Beck continued to post on TikTok anyway.

Triller certainly capitalised on TikTok's tumult. It ended up atop the app store rankings in more than 50 countries worldwide, leaping 559 places in Germany's app store in early August 2020. That was, the company claimed, because of a 20-fold increase in downloads in a week, taking it beyond 250 million downloads

– numbers that were queried by third-party monitors until the threat of a lawsuit caused them to step back and accept them. At the same time, the company claimed 65 million of those who had downloaded the app were monthly active users – around 10% of TikTok's numbers.

Triller was making every effort to point out that it was a home-grown alternative to TikTok. In June 2021 it announced plans to launch an initial public offering, seeking investment that would value the company at $5 billion. However, it was still small fry in comparison to the giant whale that also entered the market right as TikTok reached its nadir.

Mark Zuckerberg had been warning about TikTok's success for a year, ever since he told Facebook employees that TikTok was the first Chinese success story to reach outside the country's restrictive borders. He had tried Lasso with little success, but hoped another of his apps would fare better: Instagram Reels.

Reels would prove controversial. It looked a lot like TikTok. And its launch came right as Trump was shouting loudest about banning TikTok. The Facebook founder had a private dinner with Donald Trump at the White House in October 2019, when Zuckerberg reportedly made the case that Chinese companies threaten American businesses. It's a claim the *Wall Street Journal* says Zuckerberg repeated constantly in meetings with senators – around the time the United States began its national security review into TikTok.

Facebook itself categorically denies the claims that Zuckerberg is behind the US government's increased scrutiny of TikTok, calling it 'ludicrous' that national security concerns have been shaped by Zuckerberg's statements alone. But no one said that Zuckerberg alone was responsible – and Facebook and the White

House continued to refuse to say what Zuckerberg and Trump talked about over their meal.

TikTok, for its part, wasn't too troubled about the launch of Instagram Reels – at least not publicly. 'I think everyone knows a compliment when they see it,' TikTok's UK chief, Rich Waterworth told me. 'And what could be more complimentary than someone trying to replicate all the great things we've been doing?' Waterworth believed that Instagram Reels would struggle to emulate TikTok's dynamism. 'You can't copy the creative spirit that is at the heart of our community, and so we feel really confident and excited about where TikTok is going, and other people can focus on whatever they want to do.' Instagram isn't the only tech giant trying to muscle in on TikTok's turf. YouTube has also announced its own competitor, YouTube Shorts, which also comes with a similar $100 million Creator Fund to TikTok's.

Whatever happened in the conversation between Trump and Zuckerberg, and whoever was in the ear of the decision makers in the United States, the question Donald Trump had put to Americans, and to the rest of the world, was a simple one: do you want your future in the hands of the Silicon Valley giants who had spent the last quarter-century showing their willingness to run roughshod over civil rights by co-opting our data to make trillions of dollars? Or do you want to hand over all that data to China?

Those discussions have focussed on TikTok, but there's a bigger debate to be had about the future of online video. For now, TikTok has focussed on short-form video – snippets less than 60 seconds long, designed to be snacked on and consumed on the go. But as with all things to do with ByteDance, that's not the full picture. In 2021, TikTok began stretching the upper limit of videos for some creators from one minute to three minutes, much in the same way

YouTube began giving its creators more leeway for longer videos in its early days. For those creators worried about the impact three-minute videos might have on their engagement and the resultant way TikTok's algorithm might parse their content, TikTok product manager Michael Satyapor has reassuring words. 'With different video formats, I think the process will still work the same way,' he told me. 'It's still going to be on the basis of engagement' – meaning likes, comments and shares.

As well as the livestreams that have proven particularly popular on Douyin and are becoming more of a key component of TikTok, other apps in the ByteDance family could threaten the status quo of longer-form video in the West, which is currently dominated by YouTube and Netflix. In China, Xigua Video (also known as Watermelon) is a growing force and focuses on longer-form content. It combines the user-generated vivacity of YouTube with the more critically acclaimed content on Netflix. And it's growing apace, with 128 million monthly users in China alone. It's reached agreements with the BBC to broadcast some of the British company's biggest series exclusively, and runs the gamut from popular nature documentaries like *Blue Planet* to kids' favourites such as *Hey Duggee*.

Whether you think it's a deep state plot or simply the future of technology – and all the evidence suggests it's not a deep state plot – TikTok should spark a wider discussion about the direction of technology. If the first few decades of the world wide web were crafted in an American model, the future could look a lot like the way Chinese interact with technology – in more ways than one.

Nowhere is this better demonstrated than the way the UK government tried to woo TikTok during the days when its future looked most in peril in the United States. The company was casting around for a place to locate its global headquarters, and Boris Johnson's government in Westminster was eager to see TikTok pick London. The message got out, and the Department for International Trade and the Department for Business, Energy and Industrial Strategy, along with the office of the prime minister, Number 10, sought to bring TikTok's global business to Britain.

Papers were prepared and passed around civil servants in the Departments for Culture and Business respectively about the potential benefit of bringing TikTok's headquarters to the country. In March 2020, the Department for International Trade was sent out on a mission to woo TikTok executives: they sent an invitation to a Chinese investors' dinner that would be held at the swanky riverside offices of PwC in London. There, there would be the chance to hobnob with Caroline Wilson, who the invite explained 'is due to take up a very senior position at the British Embassy in Beijing.' The trade department's head of investment, Michael Charlton, was less discreet in his email to Elizabeth Kanter and Rich Waterworth, two of TikTok's top executives in Europe. He blurted out that Wilson was the British Ambassador to China designate. 'However, until the appointment has been officially confirmed by the Chinese, this information is strictly confidential and we would ask that you remain discreet.'

TikTok did remain discreet – though the information that the UK government was willing to leak the identity of its ambassador to China to a private company didn't stay secret for long. Though in the end TikTok didn't attend the dinner, the contact between the two sides didn't end. A meeting was set up for 27 April 2020, which seemingly went well. Alex Zhu, at the time TikTok's global CEO, was invited into a call with some of the government's top negotiators, and cordial emails continued between TikTok and the UK government until a June 2020 meeting – right as TikTok's crisis in the United States was reaching a crescendo.

Elizabeth Kanter dashed off an email 90 minutes after the meeting, held virtually, began on 23 June. She apologised for the meeting being 'somewhat subdued'. It seemed attitudes had changed. By July, the papers being circulated in Westminster about TikTok's planning for the future in the UK were shoved to one side. Sources within TikTok I spoke to had changed from being coy about the potential of making a home in the UK to simply changing the conversation when it was raised. Rumour and speculation was all it was, they said.

But the papers existed in Westminster. The conversations happened. The emails were exchanged. Circumstances changed, however. Anti-Chinese sentiment was building not just at Donald Trump's campaign rallies, but its echoes were reverberating through the corridors of power across the planet. The story shifted from a single app and its importance to a more fundamental discussion of the balance of tech power, now and in the future.

36
ZHANG STEPS BACK,
BYTEDANCE RACES FORWARD

At the age of 38, Yiming Zhang has it all. He has his dream. He wanted to make a company as borderless as Google – a global success, that would look beyond the limitations of being a Chinese businessman and entrepreneur. He wasn't content to slot into the system and kowtow to the state's diktats. He didn't. He built an app around an algorithm that got to know us better than we knew ourselves, and that could tap into our desires and interests in a way that few others could. And it worked. TikTok became a global sensation, growing at a rate that most entrepreneurs could only imagine for their own companies. In a few years, it's become a household name and a cultural touchstone. The company he founded that helped build it, ByteDance, is worth at least $180 billion (and rising on a daily basis).

But as Zhang sat across the digital negotiation table from potential suitors looking to take one part of the global business he built off his hands, negotiations foisted upon both parties by the US government and its China-phobic commander in chief, he must have thought that the dream had become a partial nightmare.

Stuck in Beijing because of the coronavirus, he was trying to steer the future of his company away from rocks, wrack and ruin while working on a 15-hour time difference. He stayed up all night to thrash out options from buyers of his US business during Silicon Valley working hours, then slept during the day.

He'd done everything right, he must have reckoned. He knew the Chinese internet was oppressive and tightly controlled, and had tried to walk a tightrope, keeping on the right side of the censors he disagreed with while also maintaining an openness that matched his cosmopolitan, globe-trotting outlook. He'd protested against censorship in the late 2000s, railing against China's internet monitoring agency in an angry blog post: 'If you block the internet, I'll write what I want to say on my clothes.' And yet the country he had idealised – the spiritual home of the internet, and the custodian of a vibrant, independent digital world – was telling him he couldn't belong.

He tried to make amends, embracing radical transparency, and considered selling stakes in TikTok. He contacted Microsoft executives who better knew the American way of business for guidance on how to manage the cantankerous US President and his fears of a Chinese deep state plot. Reportedly, he devoured a book written by Microsoft president Brad Smith that talked about how Microsoft kept its moral compass as the technology it helped develop changed the world. So enamoured with its analysis, Zhang had *Tools and Weapons* translated for Chinese staff at ByteDance and demanded they read it.

And yet it may still not be good enough.

As this book was going to press, on 9 June 2021, the new US President, Joe Biden, signed an executive order just like the one that started TikTok's panicked spiral into a potential fire sale a year earlier. But unlike the executive order signed by Donald Trump, Biden's missive revoked the looming threat TikTok faced.

Those within TikTok didn't breathe a sigh of relief. While Biden didn't want to continue Trump's strong-arm tactics, the revocation wasn't a reprieve. It was a warning of what was to come.

Unlike the 45th president, who wanted to will TikTok out of existence, the 46th president promised to do things by the book. Joe Biden doesn't trust China, and he wants to ensure that the potential national security risks from TikTok and other Chinese apps are truly investigated – and if a smoking gun is found, that clearer, stronger action is taken.

The barely veiled threats that typified the Trump administration, and which didn't hold up to scrutiny in court in 2020, have been replaced by a more rigorous investigation in 2021. The threat of obsolescence still hangs over TikTok. Arguably, it's never been more clearly defined.

What Biden realises that Trump didn't – and what this book tries to explain – is that TikTok fits into a wider story of tech supremacy between the United States and China. Whoever wins this battle wins the future.

It's for that reason that the US President made China a key part of the G7 summit held in Cornwall at the height of the summer of 2021. 'We're in a contest,' Biden told reporters before stepping onto Air Force One. 'Not with China per se, but with autocrats and autocratic governments around the world as to whether democracies can compete with them in a rapidly changing 21st Century.'

If Yiming Zhang thought his company was out of the crossfire, he was quickly corrected. And he's not just getting it from the US side, either. He's managed to irk the Chinese state, too.

For nearly a decade Yiming, as he asks his employees to call him, has managed to tame the fickle forces of the Chinese Communist Party and Donald Trump's scattergun approach to governance in the United States, all the while growing ByteDance from a single four-bedroom apartment with three rows of tables crammed into a living room, into a business employing more than 100,000 people across the world.

The latter is unremarkable in the weird world of tech. Silicon Valley is full of lore about the humble beginnings of the world's biggest companies. Early ByteDance employees, hunched over laptops in the apartment where the electricity sometimes cut out, were lucky even to have IKEA furniture. Amazon's desks in its early days were converted doors on makeshift legs.

But his ability to build a multi-billion business in the highly controlled country of China, where the powers that be intervene in an instant to stymie anyone or anything they deem unsuitable, is more impressive. That he's managed to chart a course through that environment, and seemingly defeat the collective forces of the US government in its attempt to put him out of business, seems improbable.

Not that ByteDance – and TikTok – hasn't come close to collapse several times. It has lost its battle to exist in India. And its existence in China has been imperilled before, because of Neihan Duanzi, the simple app where users could share memes.

For four years, the community grew, and while it occasionally poked fun at China's overly censorious society, it got away relatively scot-free – with the exception of the ban on honking their car horns. But a livestreaming component was introduced in 2016, and with it, ByteDance lost some ability to monitor and moderate the content on the platform. The userbase teetered towards the line beyond which China's state censors wouldn't let them cross – and started stepping over it. That put it in the crosshairs of the state.

First came the half-hour TV news report into the app and its immoral content, broadcast to the country in late March 2018. A few days later, the country's State Administration of Press, Publication, Radio, Film, and Television issued a decree saying that Neihan Duanzi had 'violated social morals.' It would be subject to 'rectification measures.' The writing was on the wall.

At 4am Beijing time the day after, Yiming Zhang posted a message to his vast number of followers on WeChat, a social media platform used then by roughly a billion of China's 1.4 billion people. 'I earnestly apologise to regulatory authorities, and to our users and colleagues,' he wrote. 'Since receiving the notice yesterday from regulatory authorities, I have been filled with remorse and guilt, entirely unable to sleep.' He had been thinking about the way the last few days had played out. 'Our product took the wrong path, and content appeared that was incommensurate with socialist core values, that did not properly implement public opinion guidance – and I am personally responsible for the punishments we have received.'

Neihan Duanzi was forced to close, thanks to the pressure put on ByteDance by China's Communist Party and its displeasure at the unsavoury content it saw on the app. Zhang had made a mistake: he had been gifted an opportunity by the ruling Communist Party's plans for the economy to grow his app faster than would ever have been possible in history. His background in engineering allowed him to invest energy and resources in building the company, but 'we did not take the proper measures to improve supervision of the platform, and we did not adequately do our homework in terms of effectively controlling such things as lowbrow, violent and harmful content, and fake advertising.' He had mis-stepped, and he was full of regret. He apologised to the supervisory bodies who had ordered the closure of his app.

'We ought to do better. We will definitely do better,' he concluded. 'We earnestly await help from various parts of society in supervising our rectification. We will not disappoint everyone's hopes.'

The contrition worked. ByteDance and its products have had more hassle from governments in India, Pakistan and the United States than its own in China. Until now.

In late May 2021, Douyin, ByteDance's Chinese version of TikTok, was one of 105 apps singled out by China's Cyberspace Administration – its internet watchdog on standards – for infringing users' data rights. While we in the West worry about TikTok users' information being sent over to China, the country itself is starting to catch up to the European General Data Protection Regulation, or GDPR, which imposes limits on how companies can handle personal data. ByteDance, like the others caught up in the Chinese regulator's dragnet, had 15 days to rectify the situation or face punishment.

Just two days before the Chinese state cracked down on Douyin, Yiming Zhang emailed all staff at ByteDance. 'Since the beginning of this year, I've spent a lot of time thinking about how to better drive real long-term breakthroughs, which cannot simply rely on steady, but incremental, progress,' he wrote. Colleagues of his had noticed he hadn't updated his OKRs, the goals he wanted to set himself – and which he expects all employees to do – for the next quarter. The answer, he said, was because he hadn't met the last lot of targets.

'For a long time, I've put my online status as "Daydreaming",' he wrote. 'What I mean isn't that I'm zoning out, but rather that I'm thinking about possibilities that people might think are just fantasy. In the past three years, many things that seemed like fantasies have, in fact, become reality.'

But in meetings he had started zoning out – or rather, he'd struggled to keep up. While in 2017 he was able to keep up with his software engineers as they talked about the latest developments in machine learning, by 2021 he couldn't. He had a long list of articles set aside to read later. The problem was, other things kept coming up.

Few could blame him for falling behind: the previous 12 months had seen ByteDance lose 200 million users in India overnight thanks to a government decree, and run the real risk of losing 100 million more – which, in an attempt to stop happening, had forced Zhang into meetings with the world's biggest technology companies as potential suitors. This wasn't delegated: employees told me and other journalists around the time we tried to track every squirrelly turn of the Trump brouhaha that the only person who really knew in whose ownership TikTok would end up was Zhang himself. He was the one on the calls.

At the same time, he was trying to keep a runaway minecart carrying gold worth billions of dollars on the tracks as it rolled around the world, gaining nearly 500,000 new users a day. An app that in January 2018 had a userbase equivalent to the population of Myanmar by October 2020 had enough users to people America twice over – and Germany with what was left spare. The leaders of those countries sometimes struggle to control populations that size.

So it was little wonder that he chose to step back. To replace him as ByteDance CEO, he had already handpicked a successor: the company's co-founder, Liang Rubo, who helped him set up the poky office in the residential block. 'Since Day 1, Rubo has been an invaluable partner – completing my coding for new systems, buying and installing servers, and developing key recruitment and corporate policies and management systems, among a list of contributions too long to enumerate,' Yiming told employees. He'd hand over the reins gradually in the second half of 2021, leaving him time to explore the long-term future of the company.

In essence, Zhang was too Western for China, and too Chinese for the West. He found himself lost. But TikTok isn't.

37
THE BATTLE FOR
TECH SUPREMACY

TikTok is big. TikTok is here to stay. We need to pay attention to TikTok.

But not just to TikTok alone. The reason this book broadens its investigation beyond the app to ByteDance, and the delicate discussions about the future direction of technology in the next few decades, is because it is important. Ever since Yiming Zhang picked up his first business biography, he has wanted to create a multinational company that rivals Google. He is determined that he'll do that, regardless of the fetters Chinese authorities and international politicians want to put on him. TikTok is the foothold that gives ByteDance a position of power from which to diversify and expand.

To understand the future of technology, the direction of travel, and the magnetic shift of power away from California to a more internationalist outlook, we need to understand ByteDance, its ambitions, and the pitfalls and potential that come from its ascendancy. We need to understand the tech culture that creates TikTok, and the odd unease of the outward-facing executive who recognises he has to adhere to the demands of the politicians who call the shots – wherever they are in the world.

We also need to know the tech culture that gave birth to the Silicon Valley giants. And why the rise of an app like TikTok, born in an authoritarian state that has oversight of all aspects of a business and the content hosted by it, is such a departure. The success of Facebook, YouTube and Twitter is born from a libertarian, free speech ideal; a laissez-faire attitude towards free enterprise that allowed so-called 'tech unicorns' to grow with minimal oversight. Never mind that many of the problems we face today around political polarisation, the acceptance of conspiracy theories, and the belief in fake news is a result of this hands-off attitude. It's the polar opposite of the environment that produced TikTok.

We need to know that this is about more than simply TikTok and its future: it's about the future of the apps we use, and the phones in our pocket. It's about where our data goes, and the kind of considerations we have about how that data is used.

We've spent years watching the rise of China and Chinese tech from the outside, looking at it as an alien, other way of doing things. We've had decades of Chinese-made hardware powering the devices we use. But for the first time, we're seeing the potential of technology with Chinese roots being used by everyday people, every day. The conversation is shifting. The joke that Chinese companies simply copy the latest tech innovations from the West and produce inferior versions no longer rings true. Now Chinese companies – like ByteDance, Kuaishou and Tencent – are leading the way in innovation, and Facebook, YouTube and Instagram are copying them.

'The narrative previously was about China coming up with its own versions of [Western] digital products,' says Elaine Jing Zhao, senior lecturer in the school of the arts and media at the University of New South Wales in Australia. 'Nowadays, you see the narrative shift towards how Western social media platforms are learning from Chinese social media platforms.' These superapps of Chinese origin are beginning to redraw the rules, and shape the world in their image.

The risk, according to one leading Western politician, who asked not to be named, is that the most aggressive countries pursuing Chinese apps for trumped-up fears about data handling could split the global internet. 'If we don't find a better way of answering the "What about Facebook and Twitter?" question, we're going to undermine ourselves.'

The future direction of tech, and whether it travels down a path charted by the Silicon Valley beasts, or a more Chinese-centric one, matters, the politician says. 'One of the surprising things is how social media has changed the way we live,' they say. 'For many, Facebook is the internet. For many people, news is Twitter. The algorithms these companies produce are hugely important – not the data they put on it, but what they allow you to see, even if they don't do it deliberately.' The politician is clear that they don't believe there's anything malicious or deliberate in TikTok's algorithm that is trying to press Chinese soft power across the globe.

This isn't a social media equivalent of RT, the Russian government's attempt to recast reality through its lens, or the Chinese English-language equivalent news channel, CGTN. But it does change things in more subtle ways.

'These things may be shaped by 0s and 1s, but fundamentally what you're doing is you're injecting your own views of the world into it,' the politician says. 'As you code it, you're coding in your idea of what a family is.' Think about the way Facebook redefined casual dating by putting the 'It's complicated' option into its relationship choices for users. That has spread through the planet – including its most censorious cultures. 'If these platforms are coded by kids who live in multi-dorm rooms in China, they're going to be coding in different norms,' the politician says. "It's complicated" doesn't really matter. What does matter is concepts of what it means to be private, what does private space mean, and what is the state or the company allowed to know.'

That's something TikTok has wrestled with as it tries to become as borderless as Google. It's seen in the often awkward questions the app has had to answer about its treatment of the disabled and the overweight; about its accusations of silencing Feroza Aziz, and about its different approach to women and their bodies through its algorithmic silencing. None of those are deep-seated concerns about Chinese thinking poisoning the well of Western discourse and bringing about a Communist revolution in highly capitalist countries. But there are worries about inching towards a more censorious, more regimented, more cautious reality with TikTok's every advance.

Of course, TikTok has taken great pains to unpick the Chinese origins of its app, and the cautious sensibilities of not wanting to irk the state censor that permeated it. It's a challenge highlighted in tricky UK parliamentary testimony in September 2020. Theo Bertram, TikTok's European director of public policy, said: 'TikTok is a business outside of China. TikTok in the UK is led by a European management team that has the same concerns and world views as you do.'

But, Bertram admitted, those Western executives were on a journey to remove the Chinese bias from the company. 'We know people have these concerns, and we know it's because we have this question of China hanging over us. We are committed to a higher level of transparency than anyone else because we want to prove our platform does not have any influence from China, and this is a place where the LGBT community, people with body positivity are welcome, they are protected, they are celebrated and they are lifted up.'

38
CONCLUSION

This is where I'm due to draw the proverbial rabbit out of the hat. In TikTok parlance, I've given you the set-up, I've teed up the punchline, and this is where I'm meant to dramatically cut to the payoff: the evidence of Chinese state control.

It's what a significant proportion of people want from a book like this, and what people have spent several years trying to pursue proof of. But the reality is, I can't.

I'm a journalist, whose job it is to find out facts. I have sources deep within TikTok on several continents, who have been there throughout the whole life of the company, and sources in external organisations. To the best of my knowledge, the evidence doesn't support the idea that TikTok is part of an attempt by the Chinese state to infiltrate or subvert Western democracies.

Which isn't to say that someone won't eventually find such evidence. Nor is it to say that there haven't been mischaracterisations of the way TikTok handles your data designed to discourage the more conspiratorially minded anti-China hawks from getting carried away. TikTok isn't a social media sleeper cell waiting to be activated remotely on millions of Westerners' phones.

Charli D'Amelio won't appear one morning, put down her Dunkin' coffee, and start proselytising about Mao's *Little Red Book* (at least not until college, anyway). You aren't going to find yourselves subject to a call from Chinese Communist Party members asking you to spy for them because you're spending more time than most on TikTok. Those fears can be put to bed.

But nor is the company, or the cultural stranglehold it has over us all, as innocuous as it seems. While it's not sending data direct to Xi Jinping, the fear of that has meant TikTok has glossed over some of the details in public statements that would demonstrate some data does go to China, where it could theoretically get hoovered up by the Chinese state – even if ByteDance is not a willing participant in the process. And while you won't see TikTok's biggest Western names going to bat for the Chinese president, its cultural code and content moderation guidelines, while refracted through many Western lenses by this point, still contain the nucleus of a Chinese core if you focus the microscope. That's a concern for many.

So should you worry about TikTok? Not really. At least not in the way the most corpulent, vein-poppingly angry politicians of the world suggest. There isn't a direct line between Xi Jinping and Yiming Zhang. ByteDance isn't doing the Chinese state's bidding. Just as the United States didn't seed outlets of McDonald's in the Soviet Union to overthrow communism there, so China isn't sending out TikTok as its outrider for a cultural invasion of the West. If it were, it's done a pretty bad job of it, given the hackles its existence has raised in seats of power worldwide. Even if it were the case, we are not so stupid to fall for it.

But you should be aware that TikTok's success, no matter how benign, does begin to mould the future of our technologically enhanced lives in a way some may feel uncomfortable with. We've given away most of our lives to Silicon Valley's billionaires, and relied on them not to do anything evil with it. We're now giving away our lives to someone who wants to emulate Silicon Valley's billionaires. We could, in future, give away our lives to future Chinese entrepreneurs who want to follow in their footsteps.

Yiming Zhang, after all, is now China's fifth-richest entrepreneur, worth an estimated $54 billion alone. Just as Zhang picked up biographies on General Electric's Jack Welch to learn from him, so young Chinese entrepreneurs with dreams may pick up this and other books to learn how Zhang navigated the tricky and often treacherous path between building a startup engineered for success in China, and one that can have a bigger impact – and bigger returns – worldwide.

Through the rise of TikTok, and the move towards a future defined more by companies with an origin in China and their products, we're also likely to see a shift in the way we interact with and use technology. Chinese internet users value mobile-first convenience, and the idea of the single superapp, from which they can do everything from updating their bank account to keeping in touch with friends and watching the latest entertainment. Chinese consumers, with a vibrant, burgeoning economy, prefer their digital entertainment to be live streamed more than we do in the West. That's a different world to the one in which we currently live. And it's not just TikTok that could change our lives. Other Chinese companies – and other companies from Asia – could rewrite our relationship with technology. 'Platform logics developed from China are now being extended into the Western ecosystem,' says Jian Lin of the University of Groningen, who studies China's social media platforms.

And Lin thinks these apps, and the models and modes of communication they develop, are the blueprint for the future, even discounting the geopolitical machinations going on. 'If we only talk about the business of social media platforms, I think they'll grow stronger and larger in the coming years,' he says. The strong basis they have in China is a stepping stone that gives them the financial clout to expand internationally. And they've got the implicit support of the Chinese government, which wants to see more and more Chinese internet companies go global.

'These regional giants might want to have a slice of the global market pie as well,' agrees Elaine Jing Zhao of the University of New South Wales. 'We're seeing Facebook and Google competing for a slice of the Asian market, but at the same time local giants are entering the US market as well. It's very complicated terrain, because if you want to be a global company, you're serving different consumers with different cultural tastes.'

But those cultural tastes can be reshaped over time, as TikTok's prodigious rise demonstrates. It has already given a voice to the voiceless, brought about a resurgence in certain books, musicals, and music, as well as given birth to a new generation of social media stars. It's normalised dancing in supermarket queues and on building sites, and acquainted a generation of people with the intricacies of learning carefully choreographed routines. It's shaped society at a time when we've spent more time than ever at home, alone, on our phones. According to TikTok's own polling, three-quarters of users come to TikTok to be entertained and they are 14% happier after using the app.

And those norms are being rewritten in a more globalised way. Provided we're conscious of the changes, and carefully monitor how they affect us – keeping TikTok honest, and making sure that what they say is how they act – we're likely to see big but non-damaging changes. The China hawks can continue to raise concerns about the country's encroachment on our way of life, and act as a watchdog to make sure we don't slip too far into a new normal we don't accept. The race for the future of technology is still alive, and there are multiple competitors tearing down the track – which is a welcome change, given we'd granted American tech giants a three-lap headstart, and the trust we've given them hasn't always held up to careful scrutiny.

Competition from China isn't necessarily a bad thing, not least given the efforts the company behind TikTok is making to differentiate its Western outposts from its headquarters. With careful monitoring, there's the opportunity to blend the best of Chinese tech, with the assurances and security of Western ideals, expanding the way in which we work, live and play in new directions, while keeping the fears of scrutiny from Chinese security services at bay. As with all these things, there's a need for thoughtfulness – difficult at a time when we're more tribal than ever, and sometimes live our lives in black and white, rather than in shades of grey.

My hope is that by reading this book, you'll have a more rounded view of the seismic shifts currently happening in front of our eyes, and a more nuanced idea of what that means for all of us. But more than that, I hope you'll pay attention to the app you may think is all about teenagers dancing and see it for what it is: a key driver of society, and an augur of the tech future to come.

ACKNOWLEDGEMENTS

Publishing moves slowly and social media moves quickly, which makes writing a book about a geopolitical lightning rod growing faster than no other app has done before quite difficult – even before you factor in a pandemic. Martin Hickman at Canbury Press has battled the impact of coronavirus on his personal health and his company while shepherding this book to completion. Doing such a book in 'normal times' would be hard enough, never mind now. Zoe Apostolides and Lisa Moylett helped market this proposal to publishers at a time before TikTok became front page news. Thank you to all three.

It would be rude not to thank TikTok's executives and staff, including its PR team, for giving me access to many key members of staff for interviews for this book and other reporting over the last several years. (It makes a change from other companies.) Particular thanks should be given to Rich Waterworth, who has given me more time as a single reporter than most tech executives would to the entire cadre of journalists covering their company. That said: I would still like to talk to Yiming, and would still like to get your user numbers officially – but will make do with getting the latter through other means.

Which leads me to thank the dozens of current and former ByteDance and TikTok employees who spoke to me for this book, many under the condition of anonymity because they're not meant to speak to the press. This book – and my reporting – would be much poorer if you hadn't put your trust in me as a journalist.

I'm glad to say coverage of internet culture has moved on since my last book, which means the pool of editors to thank for commissioning me to write about TikTok has grown bigger. Particularly supportive have been Shona Ghosh and Jack Sommers at Insider, who saw the value of covering TikTok's development in the last year or more. Jack has previously said a life goal is to be mentioned in at least five book acknowledgements. You now have one.

David Craig at USC Annenberg has helped not only demystify some elements of the Chinese creator economy but has proved invaluable with his industry contacts. His books on the industry are well worth reading. Countless others within the digital world have helped me throughout my reporting – far too many to mention here.

Thank you to Fraser Elliott for not just helping get me into TikTok, but YouTube too. All this is your fault. Zoe Glatt, too, is partly culpable, after dragging me to the TikTok panel at VidCon London 2019. Blame them both.

Writing a book, surviving a pandemic and continuing to work from home while spending all day, every day with a partner may be a nightmare for some, but not for me. Thank you, Angelika Strohmayer, for all you do.

And thank you to my parents and grandparents, who are slowly getting used to my name appearing in print. I'm in the position I am because of your sacrifices, care and support. They're also becoming slightly more knowledgeable of the subjects I write about. Thankfully, their pre-smartphone mobiles can't run TikTok.

NOTES

This book is the product of a combination of more than 120 on the record and background interviews and countless hours of research. Many of those spoken to are employed by TikTok or ByteDance.

The two companies themselves enabled more than a dozen interviews, only some of which are included in the references below. (Generally, significantly more officially organised interviews than are listed below provided vital background or contextual information in reporting this book.) I remain thankful to them for engaging positively with this book, and hope they feel their trust in my fair reporting has been well-founded.

However, many multiples more than that number of interviews with other ByteDance and TikTok employees in countless countries and territories are referenced here with anonymity and sometimes with obfuscation, to protect sources. That includes those both currently working there and those who have left the company during its near-decade of existence.

Likewise, to protect sources who furnished information they were not allowed or authorised to give, some sourcing (such as 'Internal TikTok user data, 2020') is, by necessity, vague. I apologise that the realities of reporting butt up against the rigour of book references.

I am indebted to a number of industry sources for the time they gave to me. Only some of them are named directly below, either because they provided background context, rather than hard facts, or because they have a working relationship with TikTok or ByteDance that they felt could be harmed by being connected to comments in the book.

Several academics who have begun research into TikTok or ByteDance products, or have studied social media in general, were also generous with their time but are not directly named here. I am energised by the existing academic literature around the two companies, and excited to see published what research is currently being conducted into them.

In short, a book like this is made possible by the collective knowledge of many brains; people like me are often little more than a translator. Listing every source and interview would distort the natural size of this book.

Introduction

- Interview with Yazmin How
- TikTok for Business Download event, June 2021
- TikTok testimony to the UK parliamentary Committee for Digital, Culture, Media and Sport, September 2020
- TikTok India user numbers, December 2019

Chapter 1

- Interview with Alex Zhu, 2016
- TikTok US court filings, 2020
- Interviews with Rich Waterworth
- *YouTube channels, uploads and views: A statistical analysis of the past 10 years*, Mathias Bartl, 2018
- Transcripts from Techbuzz China, accessible from https://www.techbuzzchina.com/bytedance/bytedance-ceo-zhang-yiming-at-tsinghua-university-part-1

Chapter 2

- *TikTok Stars are Preparing to Take Over the Internet*, Taylor Lorenz, The Atlantic, July 2019, accessible from https://www.theatlantic.com/technology/archive/2019/07/tiktok-stars-are-preparing-take-over-internet/593878/

Chapter 3

- California lawsuit against TikTok
- Facebook Australia user numbers, 2020
- Letter from Chuck Schumer, Tom Cotton and Marco Rubio to Steven Mnuchin, 23 October 2019
- Interview with Rich Waterworth
- *Revealed: how TikTok censors videos that do not please Beijing*, Alex

Hern, *The Guardian*, September 2019, accessible from https://www.theguardian.com/technology/2019/sep/25/revealed-how-tiktok-censors-videos-that-do-not-please-beijing
• *TikTok: Cheerfulness and censorship*, Markus Reuter and Chris Köver, *Netzpolitik*, November 2019, accessible from https://netzpolitik.org/2019/cheerfulness-and-censorship/
• Comments from TikTok press office

Chapter 4

• Transcript of Xi Jinping's comments to the National Propaganda and Ideology Work Conference, 2013
• *The Great Firewall of China*, James Griffiths, Zed Books, 2019
• Baptiste Robert analysis of TikTok source code, 2020, accessible from https://medium.com/@fs0c131y/tiktok-logs-logs-logs-e93e8162647a

Creator Focus: Luca Gallone

• Interview with Luca Gallone
• Famous Birthdays profile of Luca Gallone, accessible from https://www.famousbirthdays.com/people/luca-gallone.html

Chapter 5

• *TikTok Owner's Value Exceeds $100 Billion in Private Markets*, Lulu Yilun Chen, Vinicy Chan, Katie Roof and Zheping Huang, Bloomberg, May 2020
• *Bytedance Is Said to Secure Funding at Record $75 Billion Value*, Bloomberg, October 2018
• Yiming Zhang note to ByteDance employees, June 2021
• *Attention Factory*, Matthew Brennan, independently published, October 2020

- Techbuzz China podcast series on ByteDance
- Transcripts from Techbuzz China, accessible from https://www.techbuzzchina.com/bytedance/bytedance-ceo-zhang-yiming-at-tsinghua-university-part-1
- Interviews with past and current ByteDance employees
- *Intel and ByteDance Partner on AI Lab*, Synced, August 2018, accessible from https://medium.com/syncedreview/intel-and-bytedance-partner-on-ai-lab-b678036cbda4
- *Toutiao Founder and CEO Zhang Yiming Talks About Copyright Protection Measures*, Emma Lee, *TechCrunch Beijing*, August 2014, accessible from https://technode.com/2014/08/15/toutiao-founder-and-ceo-zhang-yiming-talks-about-copyright-protection-measures/
- ByteDance tour of the company's first office, posted on YouTube, accessible from https://www.youtube.com/watch?v=TIYPXpfA7_Q
- ByteDance investment slide deck, January 2013

Chapter 6
- Interview with Stewart Reynolds

Chapter 7
- Interview with Karyn Spencer
- *Inside the Hollywood Home of Social Media's Stars. (Don't Be Shy.)*, Daisuke Wakabayashi, *The New York Times*, December 2017, accessible from https://www.nytimes.com/2017/12/30/business/hollywood-apartment-social-media.html

Chapter 8
- CB Insights analysis of ByteDance
- Crunchbase profile of ByteDance
- Interview with John Bolton

- Crunchbase profile of Flipagram
- Interviews with past ByteDance employees

Chapter 9

- Interview with Alex Zhu
- *How a failed education startup turned into Musical.ly, the most popular app you've probably never heard of*, Biz Carson, *Business Insider*, May 2016, accessible from https://www.businessinsider.com/what-is-musically-2016-5?r=US&IR=T
- Interview with John Bolton

Chapter 10

- *Attention Factory*, Matthew Brennan, independently published, October 2020
- Interviews with past ByteDance employees
- Internal TikTok graphics style guide, 2021

Chapter 11

- *Attention Factory*, Matthew Brennan, independently published, October 2020
- Parallel Platformization of Douyin and TikTok by D Bondy Valdovinos Kaye and Xu Chen, 2020
- Interview with D Bondy Valdovinos Kaye
- Interview with Zoe Glatt
- Interviews with past ByteDance employees
- Interview with unnamed current TikToker
- *When Does Plastic Surgery Become Racial Transformation?*, Chris Stokel-Walker, *BuzzFeed*, 2013, accessible from https://www.buzzfeed.com/chrisstokelwalker/when-does-plastic-surgery-become-racial-transformation

Chapter 12
- Interviews with past ByteDance employees
- Interview with Geetha and Sarada Sridhar

Chapter 13
- *Attention Factory*, Matthew Brennan, independently published, October 2020
- Interview with Alex Zhu
- *China's ByteDance is buying Musical.ly in a deal worth $800M-$1B*, Jon Russell and Katie Roof, *TechCrunch*, November 2017, accessible from https://techcrunch.com/2017/11/09/chinas-toutiao-is-buying-musical-ly-in-a-deal-worth-800m-1b/
- Press release from ByteDance announcing purchase of Musical.ly

Creator Focus: Anna
- Interview with Anna Bogomolova

Chapter 14
- Interview with D Bondy Valdovinos Kaye
- *You Now Have a Shorter Attention Span Than a Goldfish*, Kevin McSpadde, *Time Magazine*, May 2015, accessible from https://time.com/3858309/attention-spans-goldfish/
- *Abundance of information narrows our collective attention span*, accessible from https://www.eurekalert.org/pub_releases/2019-04/tuod-aoi041119.php
- Interview with source with knowledge of ByteDance's hiring and expansion plans
- *TikTok's underlying tech is going on sale as a B2B product*, Chris Stokel-Walker, *Insider*, April 2021, accessible from https://www.

businessinsider.com/bytedances-new-byteplus-division-selling-tiktoks-underlying-tech-2021-4?r=US&IR=T
- Interview with Yazmin How
- Interview with Sabba Keynejad
- Interviews with current TikTok employees
- *How TikTok recommends videos #ForYou*, June 2020, accessible from https://newsroom.tiktok.com/en-us/how-tiktok-recommends-videos-for-you
- TikTok press briefing on the algorithm, June 2021
- Interview with Leena
- *TikTok influencers are telling people to stop using the app*, Chris Stokel-Walker, *Input Magazine*, February 2020, accessible from https://www.inputmag.com/features/tiktok-tips-telling-users-log-off-get-outdoors-sleep
- Interview with Colin Gray

Chapter 15
- TikTok personal usage data of Taha Shakil and Hollie Geraghty
- Interviews with Taha Shakil and Hollie Geraghty

Chapter 16
- *YouTubers: How YouTube shook up TV and created a new generation of stars*, Chris Stokel-Walker, Canbury Press, 2019
- Interviews with current ByteDance employees
- Interview with Fabian Ouwehand
- *Exclusive: TikTok-owner ByteDance to rake in $27 billion ad revenue by year-end: sources*, Julie Zhu and Yingzhi Yang, *Reuters*, November 2020, accessible from https://www.reuters.com/article/china-bytedance-revenue-idUSKBN27R191
- TikTok Creator Marketplace

Chapter 17

- Internal TalentX data for clients
- Interview with Warren Lentz
- Footage from Sway LA party, 2020

Chapter 18

- Interview with Fabian Ouwehand
- Interview with former TikTok employees
- TikTok US court filings, 2020
- TikTok press releases on Creator Fund in US and Europe, 2020
- Interview with Curtis Newbill
- Interview with numerous creators
- Interview with current TikTok employees

Chapter 19

- Interviews with Rich Waterworth
- Interviews with former ByteDance employees
- Internal TikTok user data, 2020
- Interview with Alex Zhu
- *TikTok will pay $5.7 million over alleged children's privacy law violations*, Julia Alexander, *The Verge*, February 2019, accessible from https://www.theverge.com/2019/2/27/18243312/tiktok-ftc-fine-musically-children-coppa-age-gate
- Federal Trade Commission press release, accessible from https://www.ftc.gov/news-events/press-releases/2019/09/google-youtube-will-pay-record-170-million-alleged-violations
- Interview with Dylan Collins
- *TikTok's Videos Are Goofy. Its Strategy to Dominate Social Media Is Serious*, Georgia Wells, Yang Jie and Yoko Kubota, *The Wall Street Journal*, June 2019, accessible from https://www.wsj.com/articles/

tiktoks-videos-are-goofy-its-strategy-to-dominate-social-media-is-serious-11561780861

- Public social media comments by current TikTok employees
- TikTok careers website
- TikTok callouts to creators
- Interview with Fabian Ouwehand
- Interview with unnamed TikTok creator
- Internal TikTok deck for advertising clients
- Artist Influence pitch deck

Creator Focus: Cumbermatch

- Interview with Peter Clarke
- *This Ariana Grande TikTok Impersonator is So Good She Even Has Ariana Grande Shook*, Tamara Fuentes, *Seventeen*, November 2019, accessible from https://www.seventeen.com/celebrity/a29955043/ariana-grande-tik-tok-impersonator-paige-niemann/
- Interview with Priscila Beatrice

Chapter 20

- Interviews with current and former ByteDance employees
- ByteDance employee guidelines
- *Does Huawei or Ren Zhengfei have ties to the PLA?*, Huawei corporate website, accessible from https://www.huawei.com/en/facts/question-answer/does-huawei-or-ren-zhengfei-have-ties-to-the-pla
- ByteDance career website
- Interview with former TikTok employee
- Public panel discussions by TikTok employees
- TikTok Glassdoor reviews, accessible from https://www.glassdoor.co.uk/Overview/Working-at-TikTok-EI_IE2230881.11,17.htm

Chapter 21

- Interviews with current and former ByteDance employees
- ByteDance website
- Yiming Zhang letter to ByteDance staff
- *Zhang Yiming, founder of TikTok owner ByteDance, gears up for the global stage*, Yingzhi Yang and Julie Zhu, *Reuters*, March 2020, accessible from https://www.reuters.com/article/us-china-byted-ance-ceo/zhang-yiming-founder-of-tiktok-owner-bytedance-gears-up-for-the-global-stage-idUSKBN21014Y

Chapter 22

- Interviews with former TikTok employees
- Cardi B's TikTok profile
- Arnold Schwarzenegger's TikTok profile

Chapter 23

- Various iterations of TikTok content moderation guidelines
- Interviews with former TikTok content moderators
- *TikTok 'tried to filter out videos from ugly, poor or disabled users'*, Alex Hern, *The Guardian*, March 2020, accessible from https://www.theguardian.com/technology/2020/mar/17/tiktok-tried-to-filter-out-videos-from-ugly-poor-or-disabled-users
- *Feroza Aziz: I'm not scared of TikTok*, BBC, November 2019, accessible from https://www.bbc.co.uk/news/av/technology-50582918
- TikTok trust and safety briefing for press, June 2021
- *TikTok censored a pole-dancing PhD who studies how social media silences women*, Chris Stokel-Walker, *Input Magazine*, February 2021, accessible from https://www.inputmag.com/culture/tiktok-censored-banned-pole-dancer-phd-carolina-are
- *TikTok: Cheerfulness and censorship*, Markus Reuter and Chris

Köver, *Netzpolitik*, November 2019, accessible from https://netzpolitik.org/2019/cheerfulness-and-censorship/
- 'Introducing the TikTok Content Advisory Council', March 2020, accessible from https://newsroom.tiktok.com/en-us/introducing-the-tiktok-content-advisory-council
- Interview with David Ryan Polgar

Creator Focus: Sparks and Tarts
- Interview with Danny Harris

Chapter 24
- Interview with Trevor Johnson
- Interview with Paul Hourican
- Interview with Ole Obermann
- Interview with current TikTok employees

Chapter 25
- Billboard Charts for 11 May 2020
- Interview with Jacob Pace
- Interview with Timothy Armoo
- *Inside Lil Nas X's Record-Breaking, Culture-Changing Summer*, *Time Magazine*, August 2019, accessible from https://time.com/5652803/lil-nas-x/
- Lil Nas X Instagram account

Chapter 26
- Interview with Jacob Feldman

Chapter 27
- Matthew Wilder source

- Interview with Ole Obermann
- Interview with Rolf Zuckowski

Chapter 28

- *TikTok Signs as VidCon Title Sponsor for 2021, Taking Spot From YouTube*, Todd Spangler, *Variety*, June 2021, accessible from https://variety.com/2021/digital/news/tiktok-vidcon-sponsor-you-tube-1234996376/

Creator Focus: Grandad Joe

- Interview with Joe Allington

Chapter 29

- App Annie data on TikTok usage
- Internal TikTok data
- LexisNexis data on TikTok, 2019-2021
- Charli d'Amelio's TikTok profile

Chapter 30

- Interviews with former ByteDance and TikTok employees
- TikTok India user data
- Internal TikTok India marketing slides
- *This Indian TikTok star wants you to know his name*, Snigdha Poonam, *1843 Magazine*, September 2019, accessible from https://www.economist.com/1843/2019/09/12/this-indian-tiktok-star-wants-you-to-know-his-name
- ByteDance India court filings
- Indian government statements
- Polling commissioned for this book
- Interview with Geetha and Sarada Sridhar

Chapter 31

- *TikTok Stars are Preparing to Take Over the Internet*, Taylor Lorenz, *The Atlantic*, July 2019, accessible from https://www.theatlantic.com/technology/archive/2019/07/tiktok-stars-are-preparing-take-over-internet/593878/
- Techbuzz China podcast series on ByteDance
- Opinium polling commissioned for this book

Chapter 32

- Letter from Chuck Schumer and Tom Cotton to US Director of National Intelligence, 23 October 2019
- Bill tabled by Josh Hawley, March 2020, accessible from https://www.hawley.senate.gov/senators-hawley-scott-introduce-legislation-ban-tiktok-government-devices
- Fox News interview with Mike Pompeo
- Interviews with TikTok talent managers
- Email from Amazon to employees

Chapter 33

- TikTok US court filings
- Interview with Patrick Ryan about his lawsuit
- Interviews with current TikTok employees
- Letter from Kevin Mayer to TikTok staff
- Letter from Yiming Zhang to TikTok staff
- *Trump ads on Facebook claiming 'TikTok is spying on you' reached up to 5 million Americans and targeted younger voters*, Chris Stokel-Walker, *Business Insider*, 23 July 2020, accessible from https://www.businessinsider.com/trump-campaign-spend-80000-facebook-anti-tiktok-ads-2020-7?r=US&IR=T
- Letter from Yiming Zhang to TikTok employees, April 2021

- Opinium polling commissioned for this book

Chapter 34

- Baptiste Robert analysis of TikTok source code, 2020, accessible from https://medium.com/@fs0c131y/tiktok-logs-logs-logs-e93e8162647a
- Data scrape obtained by Internet 2.0 and shared for this book
- Internal emails between the UK government and TikTok
- Interviews with sources with knowledge of UK government thinking
- Interview with current TikTok employees
- *TikTok's Ratings Moved Up to 4.4 Stars on Google Play as Google Removed Mass Negativity,* Jagmeet Singh, *Gadgets360,* May 2020, accessible from https://gadgets.ndtv.com/apps/news/tiktok-rating-india-google-play-4-4-stars-apple-app-store-2236765
- CFIUS investigation data
- Interview with high-ranking western politician
- Interviews with current ByteDance employees
- TikTok trust and safety briefing for press, June 2021

Creator Focus: Mackenzie Turner

- Interview with Mackenzie Turner

Chapter 35

- *Zynn, the Hot New Video App, Is Full of Stolen Content,* Louise Matsakis, Wired, September 2020, accessible from https://www.wired.com/story/zynn-hot-new-video-app-stolen-content/
- *Tiktok rival Kuaishou surges 160% in $5.3 billion Hong Kong debut,* Arjun Kharpal, *CNBC,* February 2021, accessible from https://www.cnbc.com/2021/02/05/kuaishou-ipo-hong-kong-shares-rise-

on-debut.html
- *Tencent-backed Chinese video app sues ByteDance unit for unfair competition*, Coco Liu, *Nikkei*, May 2020, accessible from https://asia.nikkei.com/Business/China-tech/Tencent-backed-Chinese-video-app-sues-ByteDance-unit-for-unfair-competition
- Triller press release
- *TrillerNet Plans to Go Public at $5 Billion Valuation*, Sam Blake, dotLA, June 2021, accessible from https://dot.la/triller-ipo-2653375789.html
- *Facebook CEO Mark Zuckerberg Stoked Washington's Fears About TikTok*, Georgia Wells, Jeff Horwitz and Aruna Viswanatha, *The Wall Street Journal*, August 2020, accessible from https://www.wsj.com/articles/facebook-ceo-mark-zuckerberg-stoked-washingtons-fears-about-tiktok-11598223133
- Interview with Rich Waterworth
- Bringing YouTube Shorts to the U.S., YouTube, March 2021, accessible from https://blog.youtube/news-and-events/youtube-shorts-united-states/
- *BBC Studios Sets Content Deal With China's Xigua Video*, Patrick Frater, *Variety*, April 2020, accessible from https://variety.com/2020/streaming/asia/bbc-studios-content-with-china-xigua-video-bytedance-1234588065/
- Internal emails between the UK government and TikTok
- Interviews with sources with knowledge of UK government thinking
- Interview with current TikTok employees

Chapter 36

- *TikTok's Founder Wonders What Hit Him*, Liza Lin and Eva Xiao, *The Wall Street Journal*, August 2020, accessible from https://www.wsj.com/articles/entrepreneur-who-built-tik-tok-wonders-what-hit-him-11598540993?redirect=amp&s=03#-click=https://t.co/R0BhKTR3HA

- Executive order by Joe Biden
- Remarks by Joe Biden at the G7 Summit, Cornwall, 2021
- ByteDance tour of the company's first office, posted on YouTube, accessible from https://www.youtube.com/watch?v=TI-YPXpfA7_Q
- Techbuzz China podcast series on ByteDance
- China Cyberspace Administration order, May 2021
- Letter from Yiming Zhang to ByteDance staff
- TikTok US court filings, 2020

Chapter 37

- Interview with Elaine Jing Zhao
- Interview with high-ranking western politician
- TikTok testimony to the UK parliamentary select committee for digital, culture, media and sport, September 2020

Chapter 38

- Interviews with current and former TikTok employees
- *Hurun Global Rich List 2021*, *Hurun*, accessible from https://www.hurun.net/en-US/Info/Detail?num=LWAS8B997XUP
- Interview with Jian Lin
- Interview with Elaine Jing Zhao
- TikTok for Business Download event, June 2021